MEDJUGORJE AND ME

Editor Louise Hall

Medjugorje and Me

A Collection of Stories from Across the World

the columba press

First published in 2014 by

the columba press

55A Spruce Avenue,
Stillorgan Industrial Park,
Blackrock, Co. Dublin

Cover design by redrattledesign.com
Cover image by Hrvoje Joe Topić
Origination by The Columba Press
Printed by Bell & Bain Ltd

ISBN 978 1 78218 196 5

Contents

Foreword

The mere fact that this book exists is unique in itself. Think about the one common denominator in the lives of all these contributors, to name but a few: a duchess from a privileged background, who has chosen a very different life, helping those who would otherwise have no part in her life; a young salmon fisherman from the Highlands of Scotland who has become one of the most influential people in trying to remove global poverty; a former IRA member and prisoner who now preaches a very different message; the daughter of a well-known folk singer in Ireland whose counter-cultural courage brings a new meaning in life for family and friends; a beautiful young ballet dancer whose career was destroyed by a car accident, but who finds the strength to move beyond self-pity to a new awareness of life's beauty; an Orthodox Jewish businessman, with a very different cultural upbringing, who discovers the beauty of the real presence of Jesus in Adoration; a young financial businessman, working between Hong Kong and London, who leaves it all behind to give his life to God; and a TV journalist whose own struggles have enabled him to touch the lives of many abandoned children and adults with a grace that comes from a chance encounter as a young teenager.

The list goes on, as with all the characters whose stories are found between the covers of this book. The single common denominator in these people's lives that would otherwise never cross paths is an invitation to come to a remote village in the foothills of the southwestern region of Bosnia and Herzegovina, a country on the Balkan Peninsula in South-eastern Europe.

What has happened to their lives and the lives of many millions of people since 1981 has been the source of multiple investigations, documentaries, and articles written throughout the world. Even as I write this, a special Vatican commission set up a number of years ago to investigate the happenings in Medjugorje is about to present its report, already stating that this is *not* a hoax. The full facts are yet to be heard.

As a person who first went to Medjugorje in 1986, I too have been blessed with the same graces, as I witnessed the call to conversion in my own personal life and the lives of those who travelled with me.

It was a very different place back then: remote, simple, and difficult to access. Despite this, I was deeply moved by the beautiful, trusting faith of a people who had suffered greatly in their history and were now experiencing more turmoil because God had chosen this village as a signpost for the world.

There was a lot of suspicion in the early days, and much fear, as a communist government tried to come to terms with the thousands of people who flocked to the remote hillside seeking a God whom they had taught did not exist. The threat of incarceration, punishment or death did not deter the faith and courage of the people there, and the imprisonment of their beloved parish priest only made their resolve even stronger to welcome the 'Gospa' (Our Lady) and the pilgrims in their midst.

The years that followed allowed the parish to grow in the school of Mary, but no one suspected the heartbreak and suffering that was to come in the guise of a war which had been foretold ten years to the day by the Blessed Mother to Marija, one of the visionaries. The Gospa had come as the Queen of Peace, and shed her tears for a world that knew anything but peace, even in the land that she was now visiting.

Since then, the wider world has come to know of the message of Medjugorje, and of the wider connotations of the call for peace and conversion in the hearts of humankind. Even as I write this, so many communities throughout our world are being destroyed by conflict and crime. So many hearts are broken in places like Syria and the Middle East, while Ukraine teeters on the brink of a civil war which would have enormous consequences for both the region and the rest of the world. It's no wonder that our heavenly mother is concerned for us, and wants to reach out to us with this message of peace.

The stories in this book are a timely reminder that each person is called to the same peace, to create an 'active consciousness of God' in all things that we do and say, and that we weave through our daily lives a time for prayer, fasting and reflection, so that God's peace may rest in our hearts. Only in this way can we come closer to God and all that He offers. These stories are a challenge to the mediocrity of today, where personal gain overrides the needs of the vulnerable, and where God's presence is consigned to the realm of the fairy tale.

Medjugorje is far from a fairy tale: it is the living, breathing sign of the kingdom of God on earth, where all are welcome and all are equal. God's grace is not the privilege of a chosen few, but of *all* souls who yearn to know His love and peace. Louise Hall's book is an invitation to all who dare to journey to this sacred place, where heaven meets earth, and a tiny mountain village offers new hope and healing to our broken world.

Liam Lawton,
2014

Introduction

The story of Medjugorje continues, in the hearts, minds, and in the lives of millions of people from all over the world. Over thirty-three years have passed since six young children, ranging from between the ages of ten and sixteen, first claimed to have seen a vision of Our Lady on a small hill called Podbrdo in 1981. It was the 24th of June, the feast day of St John the Baptist, and the children were living in the communist country formerly known as Yugoslavia. The children said that a beautiful woman had appeared to them holding the baby Jesus in her arms. Naturally, they ran away frightened, however they returned the next day and saw the same vision which, this time, spoke to them.

Just as the six children's lives changed forever that day, countless other lives have been affected in a profound and positive way after visiting Medjugorje. There are reports from the village of the sick being healed, and the testimonies of the pilgrims show true encounters with God – a loving God, a consoling God and an ever-forgiving God.

We can only rely on the testimonies of the pilgrims – some of whom were reluctant pilgrims, and some entirely unwilling – who at some time in their fragile lives found themselves visiting the little hamlet of Medjugorje. There, amidst the vineyards and one-time tobacco fields, we hear of a land where even the most hardened of hearts are tenderised, and where the toughest of sceptics are given food for thought. It is a place where people are educated about a God who loves everyone, no matter what they have done or where they are in their lives. The words that echo from the messages of Medjugorje are gospel messages – messages of love, peace, forgiveness, prayer and reconciliation, both with one another and also with God. In the first days of the apparitions, the visionaries asked Our Lady why she was appearing. Her reply was very simple – she had come to let the world know that God does exist.

On the third day of the apparitions, 26 June 1981, one of the most poignant messages was given to visionary Marija by Our Lady when she urged, 'Peace, peace, peace and only peace. Peace must reign between mankind and God, and between all people.' Nevertheless, some years later in the communist country, the Bosnian War erupted.

Undeterred by the communist regime and by the raging civil war, people from all over the world – more than forty million – have visited Medjugorje since 1981. The horrific war ended in 1995, the village of Medjugorje remaining untouched throughout the conflict years. Today, pilgrims continue to flock to what was once a poor, small farming village. Some go out of curiosity, some to pray for a sick relative or friend. Others go hoping to reinstate the much yearned for spiritual enlightenment they may once have had in their lives, but lost over the years.

They go to pray for others, or for themselves. They go searching for the answers to life's mysteries, and to soak up the ambiance of the village where many will say God is most certainly present. Most talk of the profound peace and true faith they have there. They say it's a place of hope, where they find deep consolation. Others talk of the spiritual healing they receive in a place where everyone is embraced, regardless of one's failings. They take the messages, firstly into their hearts, and then put them into practice in their lives. The fruits that come out of Medjugorje are incomparable to any place on this earth, and they cannot be ignored. These stories simply must be told.

It is a place where vocations are born; a place where chronic addicts find solace, hope and recovery. A place where many lapsed Catholics come home to their faith in a more vibrant and enthusiastic way than ever before. The sacraments suddenly have a true meaning in their daily lives. The gift of Medjugorje for many of these people is through the active practice of their faith. It is a renewed closeness to God, one they felt they had lost, but have found again through the messages of Our Lady.

The six visionaries tell of an incomparably beautiful woman, who appears to them following three flashes of bright white light. They say that sometimes she appears dressed in gold, particularly on feast days. Our Lady, they say, appears as a young woman with black hair and blue eyes. She wears a grayish-blue dress with a long white veil, and a crown of twelve stars sit comfortably on her head. They say that when she appears, a little piece of heaven comes with her, and that if we all knew just how much Our Lady loves us, we would cry tears of joy. The visionaries say that the lady they see is our mother and that she loves all of her children, and that we are all equal in the eyes of God. No one is left out, excluded or forgotten.

The apparitions are allegedly still continuing today, and the six visionaries are now grown-up adults with children of their own. They dedicate their lives to spreading the messages of Medjugorje and to what they feel is important for all mankind to know. On the 25th of each month, a message is given to Marija to share with the world. Mirjana, who no longer has daily apparitions, also receives a message on the 2nd of each month, which is translated into many languages for all to hear.

When I met Ivan, one of the visionaries, in Medjugorje for the 30th anniversary of the apparitions in 2011, I asked him what he felt was the most important message.

He said, 'When Our Lady speaks, she speaks to us all. She is our mother, she loves us all and we are all important to her; there are no rejected ones. She needs us to spread her message. That is why it is paramount that we realise the importance of her coming and of her messages during this moment and time we are living in.

'In a special way, I would like to emphasise the most important message, which in my opinion is the message of peace and prayer. If we don't listen to those two, then we cannot accept all of the messages that Our Lady is sending. It is hard and difficult to forgive if you do not have peace in your heart. Without forgiveness there is no healing. If there is no spiritual healing, then there is no physical healing.'

I travelled out to Medjugorje in the summer of 2012, as I had just finished compiling my first book of testimonies, *Medjugorje: what it means to me*, and was hoping Fr Svetozar Kraljevic (better known as Fr Svet) would provide the foreword to my book. Fr Svet is a well-respected Franciscan priest, who has been in Medjugorje since the early days. He had been based in New York, and when he came home to visit his family, the communists took away his passport – simply for being a priest. Therefore, the decision was made for him to stay in his home country and work in the village of Medjugorje. Fr Svet said Holy Mass regularly in St James' Church, heard confessions, gave talks in English and he also took over the running of the Mother's Village after Fr Slavko passed away.

I had met Fr Svet briefly in Ireland at the funeral of Arthur McCluskey in 2011. Arthur was a wealthy businessman but self confessed chronic gambler who lived a grandiose champagne lifestyle. He would often lose up to thirty thousand pound sterling betting on horses in any given day. After one drink too many at a family wedding one night, he made a promise that he would go to Medjugorje. Needless to say, he regretted it the next morning and tried his best to get out of the impending trip. Nevertheless, Arthur arrived in the village of Medjugorje a few months later, and although he was a very reluctant pilgrim at first, he had a spiritual and visual experience there that saw him change his life forever. After selling off a lot of his businesses, Arthur set up a charity called St Joseph and the Helpers and he dedicated the rest of his life to helping the elderly and the orphans of the Bosnian War.

I met with Arthur in Medjugorje in 2011, when I was writing features for three publications, and I invited him to come to our house and tell his story to the pilgrims. He rang me a few months later to thank me for inviting him to share his story that day, and he said that he hoped to see me in Medjugorje in many years to come. Sadly, he died the very next day. Fr Svet was just one of the many people who travelled over from Medjugorje to pay tribute to Arthur at his funeral in his hometown of Emo, Co. Laois, Ireland.

On my second last day in Medjugorje in 2012, I managed to make contact with Fr Svet, and he asked me to meet him at the priests' house. When I arrived, he was in plain casual clothes – no Franciscan robes – and he asked me if I would like to join him for the day. He told me that the Mother's Village had recently purchased a new house by the sea, about an hour or so from Medjugorje. This new house would serve as a retreat house for the orphans, a place away from the Mother's Village, and he wanted to inspect the progress of the refurbishment work. Naturally, I agreed. I was looking forward to getting to know this man, who I had heard so much about.

Only the previous day, I witnessed just one of the many so-called 'phenomena' that are reported to happen in Medjugorje. It was the 15th of August, the Feast of the Assumption, and, as Fr Svet celebrated Holy Mass at the back of the Dome, thousands of locals and pilgrims were gathering. During the consecration at the Mass, I noticed a large group of people at the front of the church, all looking up at the sky. The sun was setting, and I was curious to know what they were all looking at. Many had cameras out and were taking pictures. I turned to look up at the sky to see what was catching and holding people's attention.

The sun was setting, and as I raised my head towards the sky, I saw, what every other gathered pilgrim saw – a large crucifix formed in the clouds. It was a perfectly symmetrical, huge, white cross balancing in the sky. The orange sunset only further enhanced and illuminated its magnificence.

The following day's meeting with Fr Svet turned out to be the most wonderful day as we spoke about everyday life – our families, our work and our faith. We visited the new retreat house, and I could see the pure joy in Fr Svet's eyes as he admired the progress. We also visited the Mother's Village, where I met and fell in love with baby David. David's parents were drug addicts, and had been living on the streets when his mother fell pregnant. She delivered the baby in the hospital, and the newborn struggled to cope with the severe withdrawal symptoms of drugs leaving his tiny body. After a couple of months he was entrusted into the care of the Mother's Village, and at eight months old was thriving in this loving environment.

Later that day, we talked about my first book of testimonies and I asked Fr Svet if he would consider writing the foreword to the book. He smiled at me warmly and said, 'I would be delighted to.'

I can remember a quote from Fr Svet's own book, *Pilgrimage*, which I read some months later. They are words that I often reflect on from the point of view of people like Arthur McCluskey and the many others who have made changes in their lives after visiting Medjugorje. It read:

When God grants us the desire of our heart, it is not just because we have asked Him for it. He gives it to us, if it coincides with

His plan for our life. When our desire aligns with His will, great is our joy. Yet who is to say that He did not plant that desire in the first place?

There are many who call Fr Svet 'the eyes of Christ', and more who say that he can see deep into your soul. For me, he is a great man who epitomises everything that is right about the priesthood and religious vocations. He works tirelessly with everyone from drug addicts and their families, to children who face adversity and neglect in their lives. On the day I met with him, he told me he was going to take the day off work, however his phone rang several times throughout the day and he spent all of his time talking to people and helping them with their problems.

A place can be judged by its fruits, and Medjugorje has them in abundance. The messages of Medjugorje are for people from all walks of life, regardless of creed. For many, they look at it as a place where Our Lady is asking people to come back to her son Jesus and everything He stood for when He walked on this earth.

It is true that life is not always a smooth, easy road to travel, however what we do know from the messages that come out of Medjugorje, is that we are all important in the eyes of God. Nobody is exempt from troubles, and at the same time, nobody is excluded from God's love. It is through the testimonies in the following chapters of *Medjugorje and Me* that we can truly see evidence that what God does give to this world, is the possibility to change lives.

Louise Hall,
editor

Interview with Marija Pavlović-Lunetti

In February 2013, Marija Pavlović-Lunetti came to Ireland for a three-day visit, taking in Dublin, Cork and Tralee. People from all over the country came to hear her talk and despite her busy schedule, I was fortunate to get some time with the visionary before she spoke to over two thousand people in Dublin's RDS.

Marija is a friendly, warm person and immediately greets me with a hug. Her skin is sallow and line free, her cheeks wear a sun-kissed blush and her hair is naturally highlighted.

There had been a football match between Barcelona and Milan on the previous week, and she talks about how there was no getting away from watching the match with four boys in the house, or 'five including my husband', she jokes.

Marija's conversation is jovial and one story seems to flow effortlessly into another. We went from talking about the latest football game to talking about Scotland, and about a friend of hers who lives there but who came to Medjugorje for the first time in 1982.

'I knew nothing about Scotland,' says Marija, 'only about Scottish wool.' However, she soon admits to becoming an expert as we joke about Scottish Whiskey and the Loch Ness monster.

Her friend from Scotland is, she says, 'like my sister, and would come and stay with me for months. She loves football and would go and watch the matches in Glasgow'. I soon find out that Marija's friend is a Celtic supporter.

From here, our conversation turns to radio, and Marija talks fondly about Fr Livio Fanzaga, the founder of the station Radio Maria that is transmitted all over Europe.

It seems that life is really no different for a seer who has daily apparitions of the Virgin Mary, and for that of an everyday mother whose tasks involve running a house and raising kids, in between trying to fit in a football match or listening to her favourite radio programme.

There are so many challenges we face in modern society and, when I sat down with Marija, I asked her how she found raising four boys in today's world? After all, she has come a long way since the apparitions began in 1981, when she was a young teenager living in the small farming village of Medjugorje.

From one mother to another, I was curious to know how she juggled family life while living with her visions. She smiled warmly at me when she spoke about her children, and our conversation proved that she is living a normal life, just like every other parent.

'I had a beautiful experience last year!' she tells me.

'My young boy, he chose me as the best mother in the class!' she describes, smiling at the kind gesture from her son, which any mother would adore.

'You know, I have problems like everyone else,' she says sincerely. It's an honest statement – why would she be treated any differently or be immune to the trials and tribulations of life?

Marija talks openly and honestly about raising her teenage boys and encouraging them in the practice of their faith. She talks about how they attend Mass every Sunday, like many other families, but she admits that it is sometimes hard to get teenage boys out of bed so early at the weekend. She feels it is better to attend 'Holy Mass' early rather than late in the evening.

'It is better to do it at the beginning of the day, to start the day with joy,' she says.

'They [her children] say to me, "you know, all my friends are sleeping until Midday", and I knew I was beginning to have problems and that I needed to do something.'

So, with the natural talent most mothers possess when it comes to quick thinking and problem solving, Marija came up with the perfect solution to her dilemma: she decided to make pancakes.

'I decided to make pancakes – you know, crepes – and fill them with Nutella,' she explains to me whilst smiling at her own clever idea. 'They are ready for nine o'clock every Sunday morning. The kids love it! They smell it and all get up and get dressed. Also, when they have their friends for sleepovers, I make crepes and Nutella. It has become almost like a tradition.'

However, I found out that Marija doesn't just stop there. When she drives her son to the cinema and they are inside the car, she says to him, 'Let's make a little prayer.' They say the Guardian Angel prayer and, although the seer says that it might seem like nothing, she insists that it is important. What starts off as something difficult, she says, becomes easy and then becomes very normal.

There are so many things that are 'normal' for Marija and her family, and making the sign of the cross and saying blessings before meals is part of their regular routine. However, she admits that it can be difficult for them when they are in different places and Marija feels that many Catholics are not strong enough to be able to display their faith in public.

Nevertheless, in the eyes of the Medjugorje visionary, it is the little gestures and acts that count. She spoke of one day when she visited a school and how she had some miraculous medals on her person. She noticed a 'Mama' who looked very sad and troubled, and she gave her one of the medals she was carrying and told her to pray, and that Our Lady would hear her prayer.

'I gave her the miraculous medal because Our Lady makes miracles in peoples lives.'

One would wonder how the six visionaries have coped with such intense scrutiny over the years. I asked Marija if she felt the messages from Medjugorje are finally filtering through to people.

'We always said that Our Lady called us to grow in holiness. We try to – it is not easy, but it is our choice. To be better: better Christians, better people, better Mama.

'We try to set an example and try to make a new situation. Our Lady wants to change all the World, and we are just one little piece of this world.

'When we are better, our families are better, society is better and Our Lady likes this.

'She wants us to be more holy. We always say when we are better, our work is better – we say pro-life, pro-good, pro-help and charity. Put God in first place in your life. When you have God, He can help us and you can't go wrong.'

1

Magnus MacFarlane-Barrow

SCOTLAND

Magnus MacFarlane-Barrow OBE is the founder and CEO of Mary's Meals. Today, the charity feeds over eight hundred thousand children in Africa, Asia, Latin America, the Caribbean and Eastern Europe. In 2010, he was nominated and subsequently received the CNN Heroes award. The following year he won the Scotland Entrepreneur of the Year and was also awarded an OBE. As a teenager, Magnus visited Medjugorje with his siblings, cousins and friends, after his sister read about it in a newspaper article. Some years later, in 1992, Magnus, who was then a salmon farmer, was sitting in his local pub with his brother when an image appeared on the television screen. It showed refugees suffering from the affects of the Bosnian War. Magnus and his brother urged the local people for supplies and then drove over to the war-torn country with much needed aid for the refugee camp located near Medjugorje. This visit and future visits to other countries led to the birth of Mary's Meals.

This is Magnus' testimony.

The first time I heard the word 'Medjugorje' was at our family breakfast table in 1983.

'Look, it says here that there are reports of some teenagers in Yugoslavia having apparitions of the Virgin Mary!' my sister said from behind her newspaper. She proceeded to read us the brief news item. Having been brought up knowing about famous historical apparitions like Lourdes, and having been on a family pilgrimage to Fatima the previous year, this article prompted a very excited family discussion. It had never before occurred to us that apparitions were something that could happen now, today, in our lifetime, rather than something that had occurred in a bygone era; a bit like the stories in the bible.

'Surely,' we said solemnly to our parents, 'if there is any chance that this is true, we should go there and find out.'

To our amazement and delight they decided that we, their teenage children, should go on this mission as they were busy with running their guest house (which was also our family home).

In the end, we were joined by some cousins and friends and ten of us travelled to Yugoslavia, as it was known as at the time. We landed at Dubrovnik and hired cars to get to Medjugorje, which we knew was near the town of Mostar but we hadn't actually located it on any map. We finally found it though – despite the reluctance of the police, in the still-communist state, to give us directions.

We arrived in Medjugorje, without having planned it, just in time for the evening Mass. We were surprised by the large church in this tiny village, and even more amazed to find it completely full for a weekday evening Mass. It seemed like the whole parish was in the church, and there appeared to be very few fellow pilgrims.

Afterwards, the priest who had celebrated Mass approached us and asked us if we had anywhere to stay. We later learned that he was Fr Slavko. When we explained that we didn't have anything organised, he introduced us to his sister, who immediately invited us to stay in their family home in a nearby village. And so, our first experience of Medjugorje was of a village of faith that we had never seen anywhere before – and a village of amazing hospitality.

The few days we spent with that family, and in the village of Medjugorje, changed our lives. There were three brothers in the family, of similar ages to us and with the same passion for football. We managed to bridge the language gap by talking about Italian soccer – but we were also incredibly blessed by the fact they had a cousin from Australia staying with them who was able to translate for us. But those conversations with our new friends were about much more than football, they were interspersed with matter-of-fact accounts of the many miracles they had witnessed in the village during the last two years. One of the brothers told us that he was dating one of the visionaries.

The mixture of the mundane and familiar with the mind-blowing miracle of Our Lady's presence in this parish was staggering. Because there were almost no other pilgrims staying at this time we were invited each evening to go into the small side room in the church where the visionaries were having their apparitions at that time. We had the great privilege of praying with them until they would fall to their knees when Our Lady appeared to them and we would watch as they talked to her.

By the end of our stay none of us had any doubt that this was really happening – that Our Lady was indeed appearing here in this little village to these teenagers, who were so very clearly not making any of this up, and that she was giving them a message for the whole world. Many things moved me very deeply during that visit: the stories of miracles retold by ordinary young people; the sight of the six visionaries falling to their knees in perfect unison, transfixed by something incredibly beautiful in front of them; the faithful prayer of the local people night after night gathering to say their rosaries and attend Holy Mass. In my own heart, though, there was something even more compelling going on – something harder to put into words – a conviction that God loved me and had a plan for me. It was an invitation given by Him, to me, to choose Him.

We returned home to an excited welcome party. We were not allowed to go to bed until we told all to our parents, grandparents and some priests they had invited to ask us searching questions. They even taped our discussion. They knew this might be very important and they wanted to be sure about it.

We began trying to live Our Lady's messages, fasting on Wednesdays and Fridays on bread and water (and then staying up until just after midnight, when we would feast on enormous fry-ups!), saying our rosary together in the evenings, and reading scripture. Mum and Dad could see that something amazing had happened to us. Before this, they had to chase us to say family prayers, and now we were the ones asking them! They decided to go and experience Medjugorje for themselves, this time leaving us at home as they headed off with some friends, including a couple of priests. They were moved in ways very similar to us, and when they returned home they began to feel that God was asking them to give their guest house, our family home, to Him.

They began to block out some time from the normal paying guests (who until then had normally come to fish for salmon and hunt deer) and to organise retreats. Our largest room soon became a chapel and after some months, Craig Lodge, the guest house, became Craig Lodge Family House of Prayer. Our bishop (of Argyll and the Isles) gave us the biggest gift of all, by granting permission for the Blessed Sacrament to reside in the chapel, and soon, almost every weekend, retreats were taking place, led by various priests. Some of these retreats were about Our Lady's messages, and some were about other aspects of Christian life – scripture retreats, healing retreats, etc.

Meanwhile, another development took place at Craig Lodge when some young people, returning from the first youth festival in Medjugorje, asked to form a community. Soon the 'Krizevac Community' was born, consisting of young people committing one year of their lives to try and live Our Lady's messages. In time, a permanent community – Craig Lodge Community – was also formed when a small number of families living around Craig Lodge decided to support each other in living the messages and supporting the work of Craig Lodge Family House of Prayers. All of these things continue to develop and flourish at Craig Lodge today.

Meanwhile, without having ever planned it, my own life changed forever in 1992. By then I was twenty-four years old and had for some years been a salmon farmer, living near Lochgilphead in Argyll. One weekend my brother and I were having a drink in our local pub and talking about a news bulletin we had seen that night. It was a very moving report on refugees suffering near Medjugorje (the Bosnian War was raging by this point) and we began discussing the idea of doing something very small to help. Within days we had launched a little appeal asking people to donate food, clothing and other items urgently needed in Bosnia and Herzegovina. About three weeks after that initial conversation, we found ourselves driving across Europe in an old Landrover, packed to the roof with donated goods. We arrived in Medjugorje and delivered the aid to a nearby refugee camp; left the Landrover there, as it was also urgently needed to deliver aid into the mountains, and flew home almost immediately in order to get back to our jobs.

I thought I had done my good deed, and that life would continue as normal – but God had a completely different plan! The aid we asked for continued to pour into our family home. Mountains of clothing and medical equipment and food filled my father's sheds and people continued to turn up at our door with cars and vans bulging with more donations. Cheques too were arriving in the post every day. I prayed about it and decided to give up my job and sell the small house near the fish farm at Kilmartin so that I could continue to drive out the aid. None of this was a huge sacrifice, as I was at the stage in my life of wanting to do something different.

At that age I was living two separate lives. I had never lost my faith, and was still trying to live the messages of Our Lady by saying my daily rosary, fasting and going to Mass. But most of my free time was spent drinking and partying, surrounded by others who were also living that lifestyle. I lacked peace. I knew that God was not at the very centre of my life, and that I needed to choose Him in a new way. Giving up the house and the job were not really what this decision was about: at a deeper level it was a way to try and make a new life for God. Another fresh choosing of Him over other things; something which Our Lady asks us to do every day and which I so often fail to do.

And if I thought for one second that I was giving God anything, I would soon discover He was about to shower me with unimaginable gifts. Within a few months, I received the first and greatest gift of all: I met my wife Julie, the mother of our seven children. She was a nurse in Inverness who felt God was asking her to help in the hospitals of Bosnia and Herzegovina, and who eventually began driving trucks with us, carrying medicines and medical equipment. When we went to sit our HGV tests – so we could drive the larger articulated trucks – she passed first time, whilst I failed! Over the next three or four years we delivered millions of pounds worth of aid to people suffering because of that war, and then we started being invited into other countries to help. For example, in Romania we began working with children who were HIV-positive and who had been abandoned in hospitals. We opened homes there, and today many of those children are healthy young adults. We also began working with missionary priests in places like Liberia, Peru and Colombia.

In 2002, the work that I believe God was preparing us for – Mary's Meals – was born in the most incredible way. That year there was a terrible famine in Malawi, and we watched depressing news bulletins explaining how thousands faced starvation. Back in Craig Lodge we began discussing how we might help the people there. As always, we tried to think of someone in Malawi whom we might know and who we could work with, and the only person we could think of was a lady called Gay Russell.

Twenty years previously, when we came back from that first visit to Medjugorje as teenagers, my sister Ruth wrote an article about our experience that was published in the *Catholic Herald*. Thousands wrote asking for more information and one of the correspondents stuck in our memory – Gay Russell from Malawi, who described herself as an air pilot. Mum wrote to her a couple of times and we never heard from her again – but she remained in our memories, and became a bit of a family joke as we conjured up an image of this lady flying around Africa distributing Medjugorje leaflets out the window as she went!

Incredibly, at the time we had contacted Gay, an English business-man called Tony Smith was on retreat at Craig Lodge for the first time. He told us that he knew Gay and was in the middle of a project with her to build a replica Medjugorje in Malawi (today, the project is complete, along with replica Krizevac cross, and stations and St James' Church – a place of pilgrimage and prayer for thousands of Malawians who cannot afford to travel to Europe). So Tony put us in touch with Gay, and Ruth and I travelled there to meet her and various others.

I will never forget the first evening we met Gay and her husband. After talking for some time, hearing how her life had changed after hearing about Medjugorje through Ruth's article, and about how there was now a large Medjugorje movement in Malawi, Gay opened a cupboard and took out the letter that Mum had written to her twenty years before. She even had a little faded photograph of Ruth and me with the visionaries in 1983! She also explained that she was deeply involved in famine relief work with a network of priests who were working desperately hard to keep their parishioners alive. So we began working with them, using the donations we were receiving to buy food for the worst-affected villages.

During the course of that work, two things happened that led to the birth of Mary's Meals. Firstly, I met a family whom I will never forget. A local priest led me into a small mud-brick hut on the edge of parched fields. As my eyes adjusted to the darkness inside, they introduced me to a woman called Emma, who was lying on a mud floor. She was surrounded by her six children; the youngest of them lay cuddled against her. She was forty-one years old, had AIDs, and was dying a painful death. Her husband was already dead – killed by the same disease. Like most there, she could not even hope to find the money required for medication, or even painkillers.

When I began speaking to Emma she said, 'There is nothing left for me but to pray; to pray for my children. I don't know if my relatives will be able to take them in when I go.' Already the family was reliant on the generosity of neighbours and on feeding programmes to survive. I then began talking to her oldest child, Edward, who was about fourteen years old. I asked him what he wanted most in life.

'To have enough food and to be able to go to school one day,' was the extent of his hope and ambition.

Repeatedly, whilst working in some of the world's poorest communities, we found that the very poorest children were missing school as they battled to survive; working, begging, scavenging for their next meal instead of sitting in class. They were therefore missing out on their education – their one possible escape from poverty. This encounter with Edward really brought this horrible cycle of poverty into a sharp focus. And then something else happened.

Tony Smith, the gentleman from England who had reintroduced us to Gay, was in Malawi at the time, working on the building of the replica church with Gay. He shared with me something that had happened to him. He told me how one evening in Malawi, when he had been feeling very depressed about the poverty around him, especially the suffering of children; he sat down and turned on the TV in Gay's house.

He then found himself spellbound as he watched an interview in which US Senator James McGovern passionately outlined his belief that providing daily school meals to the three hundred million hungry children of the world could be the 'catalyst to a modern-day Marshall Plan for economic development in developing countries'. Senator McGovern helped found the World Food Programme, which now feeds millions of children through school feeding programmes, but despite his best efforts the international community is still only feeding a tiny percentage of the world's hungry children. Tony felt inspired – if such a movement was consecrated to Our Lady and called Mary's Meals, it would become a reality!

When he shared this with us, we felt very deeply in our hearts that this was the work that God had been preparing us for, and before the end of the year this new work had begun in Our Lady's name. In a small number of schools and nurseries in Malawi, we began working with local communities to provide daily school meals for hungry children – with local volunteers doing all the daily cooking and serving of the food which we bought, delivered and monitored the use of. Immediately we could see that this was not just a nice idea but something that would really work. Many children who had never been to school before began coming, because they knew they would be fed. And children who used to attend school only now and again, because of sickness and the need to work for food, began coming every day. Before long other schools began asking us for Mary's Meals and we said yes and so it went on and on.

In the ten years since Mary's Meals was set up, it has grown in an incredible way around the world. As I write this, over eight hundred thousand children receive Mary's Meals in sixteen different countries, and nearly every week that number grows. This work is supported and made possible by a global movement of generous supporters. I think of Mary's Meals as a whole series of lots of little acts of love – no one doing anything spectacular as an individual, but when put together, all these kindnesses are really changing the world.

So while the HQ of Mary's Meals is still in the little tin shed that I borrowed from my father thirty years ago to store aid for Bosnia and Herzegovina, and in which I still work, there are now Mary's Meals organisations in countries such as Ireland, Germany, Austria, USA, Canada, Italy and many more. In Croatia, a group of people who used to distribute and sometimes benefit from the aid deliveries we made there during the war, now organise incredible fundraising activities for Mary's Meals. They tell us that it is good to know how to give and to receive. Nearly all of these groups have been set up by people whose lives have been changed in Medjugorje and who often hear about Mary's Meals when they visit our little information point there, or meet Milona von Habsburg, who is based there and who has devoted many years of her life to the mission of Mary's Meals.

I believe Mary's Meals is a fruit of Medjugorje. A fruit of prayer and conversion. I believe it is a beautiful, simple, motherly work of practical love. I believe it is a work of God and of Our Lady, and I pray that it continues to grow to reach many, many more hungry children.

We return often to Medjugorje. It is a blessing to see my children (the oldest now the age that I was when I first visited) feel so at home there that they do not want to leave.

What does Medjugorje mean to me? I find it almost impossible to put into words. I think of Medjugorje as an invitation and as a gift. There, I feel personally invited by Our Lady to choose God and the path of daily conversion. And there, too, I feel God gives me the grace that encourages me to try to follow that path, no matter how often I fall. I feel like I taste little bits of heaven in Medjugorje, and a profound peace that make me want more. It makes me desire holiness, even while it helps me see my own sinfulness. Medjugorje points us to Jesus, our Lord and Saviour.

If you would like to know more about Mary's Meals or get involved, you can log onto www.marysmeals.org.

2

Milona von Habsburg

ARCHDUCHESS OF AUSTRIA

Milona von Habsburg-de Rambures was born into royalty, but, from a young age, she always questioned social divides. In 1984, she came to Medjugorje for the first time, and had a spiritual experience on Cross Mountain. There, she encountered God's love and the real meaning of life. Soon after she returned home, Milona made the decision to move back to Medjugorje, where she worked as an interpreter for Fr Slavko. Milona is married with one child, and she travels the world working as an Ambassador for the Mary's Meals Charity.

This is Milona's testimony.

My full name is Monika-Ilona von Habsburg, Archduchess of Austria, Imperial Highness. I was born in Munich on 14 September 1958. My father left his homeland, Hungary, and went into exile in Portugal with his parents, brothers and sisters during the Second World War. My mother comes from a German family, and her mother was from Italy. Today, my parents live in Portugal. My brothers and sisters live in different countries across Europe and Australia.

Living in varied countries, with people of different nationalities has always been normal for us. We therefore all speak a few languages, and have been able to adapt to very different circumstances.

I am the oldest of seven living children. Our eldest brother died when he was only one day old.

I never felt privileged or above any other human being. It was God's will for me to be born in this social circumstance and I did not choose it. I did not have a virtue or a greater dignity than anybody else in this world. I lived it very simply – as a reality.

31

Being the daughter of a refugee allowed me to understand much about life and its passing character. In his early teens, my father had to change country, abandon his homeland, and begin a life on foreign ground in Portugal. His family had to go through hardship on all levels. Only people who have been forced into exile can understand how this feels.

We soon learned that we could not live in order to *have* everything on a material level. We also knew that it was not necessary. As young people it was not always easy, as we were in the midst of many who lived a very different lifestyle; taking many things for granted.

We were also practicing Catholics. We went to Mass on Sundays, and had an evening prayer with the family. I remember the flower decoration we used to have in May, in order to honour Our Lady.

From childhood, I wanted to know the deep meaning of our life here on earth and what it was all about. The first decisive moment happened when I was fourteen or fifteen years old. It did not happen in a glorious moment but as I was walking home after a forbidden ride on a friend's motorbike and having smoked a forbidden cigarette. During my walk, I lived an unexpected moment with Jesus:

'Jesus, if you were not born, then all these social differences have a place, as man has to organise his world. If you did come to this earth, which I believe, then there is one love for all, one value for all, one baptism for all, one Saviour for all. And no more difference in value and importance among human beings on earth. We all live together and work together. You did everything for man, and man is the most precious treasure for you. My path will be to come to know as many of your human beings as possible in this world of yours. This is how I will come to know you.'

Little did I know.

Ten years later, I landed in Medjugorje. I was twenty-five years old. My cousin organised a pilgrimage with three buses of relatives. We slept in two big tents belonging to the Order of Malta, in the little woods next to the church. It was the third anniversary of the apparitions, 24 June 1984.

I do not remember everything. I remember hearing about fasting, which ended in eating a whole packet of delicious biscuits. I remember climbing Apparition Hill and resting under the big nut tree in the fields on the way back.

I remember praying crowds, a full church, being thrown out of the tents by the police, and having to sleep in the grass behind the church, with locusts flying around us. We had no bathroom. We had the vineyards behind the church. We had a trickle of water at the side of the parish house.

The moment of my life changing encounter is what stays with me for ever. We went up Krizevac early in the morning. The group travelled fast. I felt a heavy weight coming down on me, hundreds of kilos heavy, which made me incapable of taking another step. I sat on a rock, looking down into the valley, seeing the church which seemed small amidst the tobacco plants and the vineyards. It was hot and silent. Someone was hammering in the far distance. I could only hear the noise of the heat, buzzing insects and chirping crickets.

Suddenly, I was not alone. A gentle presence wrapped itself around me like a mantle. She was alive, looking at me from above or behind, I could not tell. I could not see, nor hear, but I felt alive, and could hear inside of myself.

There was a gesture, indicating the valley. Eyes looked into me, making me feel a total acceptance of who I am. I was surrounded with peace, gentleness, and a fullness which gave me total comfort. She looked at my life, knowing it, but not criticising, threatening, or accusing; just looking at it as it was.

Three questions were put to me, questions which revealed their answers.

ONE: 'If this here, the happening in this valley, is true, then how could you ever call yourself a Christian?'

Well, I knew it was true, as I had felt the deep calling in my heart and my conscience to come to Medjugorje where she was expecting me. 'She is there, I must go,' had been the words echoing inside me, motivating me to dedicate myself to that trip.

In that moment, this truth became a light which showed me that I had never begun to live a full life as a Catholic Christian. I was practicing, had knowledge of the catechism, received the sacraments regularly, and loved all of it, but I lived a life that was different to the word of God. Monday was always the same again. Sunday was a breath of fresh air; a fleeting moment of joy and peace before the waves of worry and fear of tomorrow's unfinished homework collapsed over me, drowning me every day. I knew what I was not allowed to do, but I did it anyway, and wondered where my life was going.

TWO: 'Who is the God you say you believe in?'

Who God was had never entered my heart, mind or thought. He was important; I loved and defended Him before my friends who did not believe in Him or the Church, the pope, etc. In that instant came an all-embracing, all-encompassing and all-fulfilling presence, which surrounded both myself and the one who was enveloping me.

The air was filled with Him. We were breathing Him in, as He was filling every molecule with His life and presence. The fulfillment was complete. No words in this world can describe the fullness, the contentment, the stillness, and the life at that time. It was a joy, deeper than my own heart and being. There was also peace. I could give a litany of words which speak of a spark of Him.

THREE: 'Does *this* God really exist?'

Well, there he was, all around me. He was looking down and I felt his gaze; warm and alive – boy, does He exist. It seemed to me that He wanted an answer. He seemed to want something back which I took from Him. It felt as if I had stolen it from Him. It was myself, and my life. I had taken it all into my own hands, lived it according to the rules and norms of aristocracy, Pink Floyd, Easy Rider, Kings and Queens, and all sorts of little idols.

Now the time had come when He wanted to be my Father, my God, my everything. He had a plan for my life, and only He knew it. I became new under his gaze. I was seen for the first time, consciously, by Our Lady and by God.

In this fullness, I looked down on the parish church, and saw it open, without a roof. The sky turned golden and there was a movement between the open church and the sky. It moved up and down; gold and white light. It was alive. It all flowed into the open church like golden fluid. It was as if the church contained the whole of heaven.

I was sitting alone again, everyone around me had gone. The church had its normal roof. There was silence and the buzz of crickets.

All of nature's sounds were there. Never again would my life be the same as before. I had been seen.

I did not know my name, where I came from or where I was going. Nothing mattered, I was just there on the rock. No move was possible. I did not know how to move, or where to move to. My relationship to creation had changed. The ground felt different. I did not know the way up to the cross.

I saw a Roman collar on a man. He was climbing, and I stood up. I asked him in English: 'Father could you help me up the hill?'

He looked at my full height and said, 'Follow me.'

These were the first words of my new life. I was twenty-five years old, very autonomous, well-travelled, multilingual, but entirely dependant on this man, a priest whom I had never seen before.

I looked only at his feet, carefully putting my own feet into every step he took. All the way up the mountain, I only looked at his black leather sandals. There were many rocks, steps to an unknown destination.

When I looked up, there was the big white cross towering above us.

I did not know how to live the next moment, so I asked.

'Father, may I confess?'

Well, there it came.

After twenty-five years of feeling exiled, I had finally returned home. All the pain of searching for love, longing for peace, waiting for truth, seemingly in vain, came over me. I had stopped crying a while ago, and that day I could open my heart in truth and let everything out. When the father gave me absolution, my heart was breathing the fresh air of forgiveness, filled with the perfume of mercy and joy. A new life had begun. I flew down the hill, light, happy, and a new road opening up before me.

During the rest of the pilgrimage, I saw two more signs.

The cross on Krizevac turned a bright, shining white. It turned itself around, and was standing on a golden globe. It seemed to show how the light of the glorious cross was transforming the world into something precious and new.

I also saw the sun changing colour, and I could look into it. The colours of the rainbow were all around it. It seemed to spin very quickly, moving closer, and then back again.

Both signs were like a wink saying, 'Do not lose and forget what you received on the hill.' They sealed the veins of my heart with a seal of love.

A new path began; conversion is forever. For one year, I came every month, with family and friends. After that, I began helping in the parish: translating mail, travelling and assisting Fr Slavko. The visionaries became my life. I prayed and allowed the inner change to continue, which still happens today.

The war came in 1992. I met my husband Charlie, and we got married in 1996. We have a lovely daughter, Clara. We moved back to Medjugorje a few years ago.

In 2004, I began working for a beautiful fruit of the message of peace: Mary's Meals. In my personal experience, this service is in keeping with everything I learned through Medjugorje. Every person is important and wanted and loved by the Creator. We can help by trying to live that love, so we can also give love.

How? Pray, fast, confess, participate in Holy Mass, adore the Blessed Sacrament, pray the rosary, and read the Bible daily. Live it; live the messages. Serve the poor.

What does Medjugorje mean to me?

Through Medjugorje, I discovered that a life lived with Our Lady and our God becomes an adventure. It is both a school and a new challenge every day.

3

Mark Lenaghan

NORTHERN IRELAND

Mark Lenaghan grew up in Belfast, Northern Ireland during the height of the Troubles. At an early age, he became involved with the paramilitary organisation, the IRA, and was put on active service within the unit. On Valentine's night in 1982, Mark was ordered to shoot at a British army patrol. When a British soldier was injured, Mark was arrested, interrogated and sentenced to prison for twelve years. During his time in Crumlin Road prison, Mark met a priest called Fr Paddy, who told him about Medjugorje.
This is Mark's testimony.

I was born in 1960 and grew up in Belfast, Northern Ireland. We lived in a mostly Protestant and Loyalist area but our family was Catholic. However, before the Troubles started in Northern Ireland, we all mixed freely with each other, and there were no issues or problems with us being of different religion. When the Troubles eventually kicked off, we were very vulnerable living where we were. I can remember a particular attack on my family, when I was only eleven years of age, which left a very deep impression on me.

It was 1971, and our house was attacked by a loyalist gang. They had placed a bomb between our home and another, and when it went off we took the brunt of the blast. There was a nurse who lived in the other house and she was very lucky to escape with her life. At the time of the blast, I was up in the attic and the windows were blown in. I can remember my parents running up the stairs to see if I was safe.

My mother told me a story of a time when an army commander came into our area and ordered that our families be protected. However, during the height of the Troubles, those protecting us were pulled away to another area, and it left a vacuum for the loyalist gangs to come in and drive us out of our homes. We had lost everything and became almost like refugees.

There were certain things which always stuck out in my mind growing up, and the death of my teacher, who had taught me the tin whistle, was just one of them. He had been mistaken as a gunman and was shot dead by a soldier on the Falls Road. He had been hiding behind a wall when a soldier saw him and thought he was the sniper who had opened fire on the army.

We then moved to west Belfast, and there was a huge amount of rage amongst young people growing up there. We were resentful towards the army and we blamed them for losing our homes. This was fuelled by everyone else who moved to the area and who suffered brutality. Bobby Sands (the hunger striker) was just one of the people who moved from his home to west Belfast, and we saw this as the British moving in and invading our land.

As a young boy, I was very interested in history and politics. I became a member of the Fianna and got involved in riots from as young as twelve, where we would take on the army and throw stones at them. I got deeper into politics in the 1970s, and this was around the same time as the prison protests. In 1976, the 'H Block' protests began and there were many marches along the streets. I was involved with all of this but still wanted more, and so I joined the auxiliary IRA as a volunteer. It wasn't an active service at fighting the army, but we tried to keep control of areas where there were no police. People from different areas were actually coming to us for help and asking us to be the police to protect them. We dealt with those who were using drugs, stealing cars and breaking into homes.

I was involved in punishment beatings and punishment shootings, even in the early days. There was a part of me that didn't enjoy doing what I did but at the same time, I felt that I had to do it. It wasn't in my nature to do those things, but it was a role I had taken on and I felt I was defending and representing the community.

As time went on, I really wanted to move from the auxiliary unit into the active unit. I kept asking people within the organisation if I could get involved and they said they would enquire for me. Then one day, I was told that I was going to the training camp. A group of us went off and were trained with rifles and hand guns and when my training was finished, I was put in an active service unit within the IRA.

The role of the volunteer was to be available at any time and I can remember an old man talking to me one day and saying to me, 'Look, you are either going to go to jail or die. You will lose everything if you join the IRA. Is that what you are prepared to do?' My reply was, 'Yes, I have no problem with this.'

In 1981, the hunger strikes had started and in May of that year, the Troubles were really at their height. There was this rage inside everyone and we wanted to take out or kill as many people as possible.

On Valentine's night, in February of 1982, on the Falls Road, I was a shooter, and we stayed up all night waiting for an army patrol to come down. We were ordered to wait until they got to the bottom of the Falls Road at the junction and then to open fire. As we were firing shots, this guy ran across the road in front of the army jeep. I didn't realise it at the time but he had been shot and was badly wounded. I was on the back of a motorbike and as we drove closer, I could see it was a British army soldier down on his knee. The guy who was driving the motorbike revved the bike so high that it went up in the air. It hit the path and we both fell off. The rifle had fallen under the bike too and although the driver got up and got away, I was caught and arrested.

They brought me to Castlerea Prison, and I was interrogated for five days. I was so dedicated to the IRA at that time that I gave them no information but my name and address. Initially, I was charged with five attempted murders, possession of weapons with intent to kill and possession of weapons under suspicious circumstances. At the time, I was attending Queens University, and was only three months away from my final degree. My whole world caved in, and although it was a very traumatic experience, I was still very dedicated to the IRA.

I was sent to the Crumlin Road prison, and on my first night there I can remember seeing all the other prisoners looking up and staring at the new guy. I just walked into the centre, picked up a set of darts and began throwing them at the dart board. They all joked about it after saying I had a real brass neck!

My time in Crumlin jail lasted from March 1982 until January 1984. There was a period in between where we were brought up to the 'H Block' in Long Kesh prison for about six weeks and then returned again by helicopter. I should have spent twelve years in prison, as that was my sentence but I believe it was my mother who helped me see my early release.

She prayed so hard for me and when I was living at home, she used to drop holy medals and prayer cards under my bed or put them in the pockets of my clothes. It was only when I looked back many years later that I realised what I had put my family through, but my mother never gave up hope, and she prayed so hard for me. I never really considered my family, or the impact my actions had on them. It was all about me and what I was doing – I was so blind and unconscious to it all.

Although I was in jail, I still hadn't left the IRA. The prisoners became even more dedicated to the cause, as when they came into the prison they were surrounded by like-minded souls.

In Easter of 1983, I was in the 'H Block' and a priest called Fr Paddy Kelly came up to the jail. He was just one of several priests who came into the prison every Sunday. Fr Paddy would say the Mass, and then the inmates from all the different wings would come together. It was an opportunity for people to swap messages and meet other people that you couldn't meet on a normal day. Fr Paddy stood up in Mass and gave a talk, and he had this wonderful presence. He had been a Mill Hill missionary and was the parish priest of St Mary's in Belfast, and he had also been to Medjugorje.

While he was talking, he told us that he had been to this great place, which he described as a place 'of grace, forgiveness and mercy'. He said Our Lady was calling us to this place. I will always remember the phrase he used from Isaiah 1:18: 'Though your sins are like scarlet, they shall be like snow.' There was something about this phrase that was very symbolic to me. Maybe it was the red representing the bloodshed and guilt.

However, I went up to him after Mass and I was thinking to myself, 'I will convert this guy over to our cause long before he converts me to his.' I said to him, 'Father, you are talking about forgiveness and healing but we know what we are doing here, and we don't need to ask for forgiveness.' Fr Paddy let me go on talking and he just listened. When I was finished, he told me that he would be back the following week and I could tell him more then. I felt if I had a few weeks with him that I could sort him out!

Fr Paddy listened to me over the next few weeks, and when he did interject, he would have something poignant to say which gave me food for thought. I was then introduced to Fr John Murphy, who was the prison chaplain, and, over a period of months, I found myself attending Mass and listening a lot more to what they were saying. After a while, I found myself taking the Missalette and putting it in my pocket. I would then go back to my cell, cut out the scriptures and keep them. Even though I was in jail with twenty-five IRA men and subject to the peer pressure, there was something inside me that wasn't comfortable with certain aspects of it all. There was a space or an area inside me that was slightly receptive to what the priest was saying. I knew there was something else out there and that what we were doing was hurtful. It wasn't wholesome and it wasn't going to bring us any healing. Also, it would never bring us to fulfilment or happiness.

Fr Paddy talked to me about Medjugorje and what was happening there, and about the messages. He talked about the peace and the prayer, and left me some booklets about the place. I can remember he gave me a photograph of the six young visionaries who were ranging from between the ages of ten and sixteen. They all looked so young, fresh-faced and innocent, and they were staring upwards. I can remember looking at their faces and thinking to myself that they couldn't be lying. They were too pure; I felt they couldn't possibly be faking it.

As I continued to read the books about the messages, something strange began to happen. As you read the stories of the Bible, you meet broken characters. You meet the blind man, the paralysed man, and the dead man. I felt as if Jesus was coming in and offering me life, hope, grace and salvation. This happened to me very gently over a period of weeks and months. I found myself reading the scripture and feeling that I was the blind man, I was the paralysed man, and I was the dead man. I felt that the characters were me and I began to realise that I was a very broken person.

I never knew about the rosary, and I suddenly found myself reading booklets about it and then praying it. I got more books and began doing the full morning breviary. I read scripture and found out about Lourdes, Fatima and Padre Pio. One memory that sticks in my head is of mopping the prison floor and reciting the third glorious mystery in my head. Slowly, there was a transformation in me and I didn't feel any fear. Here I was, one guy in a prison wing, with twenty-five other IRA men, turning to religion!

The canteen in the prison had an IRA library. I approached the guy in charge and told him I was putting some books in the library. He asked me what they were about and so I told him they were about Medjugorje. He looked at me quite funny but told me to go ahead. I had a visit from my mother and when I came back from it, one of the inmates had told me that my books were in the bin. He told me who was responsible and so I marched straight down to him and asked him if he had put my books in the bin? I said to him, 'You talk about a democratic society and a society of freedom but there are certain people's books that you don't like!' I told him to get the books and put them back, and he did. I had this strange, mysterious courage.

I had been a ritual Catholic in that I went to Mass, but it had no real bearing on me. However, my faith began to transform inside of me. The hatred, bitterness and revenge began to leave me. It didn't happen instantly and I didn't 'see the light' in a split second; it was a very gradual process for me. Some of the guys on the wing were very receptive, and they too read the messages. Some even went to Medjugorje when they got out of prison.

About six months after I got out of prison, a wonderful priest called Fr Aidan Carroll gave me a ticket to go to Medjugorje. When I arrived there I felt I had died and gone to heaven. I had discovered so much adversity in the IRA jail and here I was suddenly in a place where everybody was happy and walking around with rosary beads. I can remember meeting Marija, the visionary, one day and she was talking about heaven and what it was like. She talked about meeting all these people in a beautiful place where they were happy and at peace and wore different coloured robes. At the time, I thought it was a bit strange as my idea of heaven was sitting in a pub with a nice pint of Guinness!

Later that night, I was walking by St James' Church and the doors were wide open. Fr Slavko was inside doing Benediction. The Blessed Sacrament was exposed, and as I walked by, the air was warm and the crickets were chirping in the background. There was silence and then prayer and I was drawn into the church. I knelt down with everyone else and closed my eyes and really experienced a beautiful sense of peace. Instantly, I understood what Marija had been talking about.

One day during my visit, a friend of mine came up to me and told me there was an ex-soldier in the village and asked me would I like to meet him. She told me he was with an English group and that he had heard about me and wanted to meet with me. I went down to meet him and we both shared our stories. I found out he was a British soldier. He had been young and unemployed and had joined the army as a profession. As a young man, he had a bad attitude, but in his personal life he was very wounded and broken, just like I had been. However, he had a huge conversion too, just like me. I asked him where and when he had served. He told me it was in 1982, in west Belfast. I told him I had been in the IRA that same year in west Belfast and that I was sure he would have shot me and I would have shot him. Yet there we were, meeting together in peace in Medjugorje.

When I came out of jail, I didn't know what to do with myself. It was all quite traumatic again. I went to Mill Hill and I was with the priests for a while, however I felt it wasn't quite for me. The inclination towards teaching came to me, and somehow I got the money together. I applied to Maynooth College to do a H.Dip. but I was told the registration date was over and that all the places were taken. I sent off my application anyway and the following week I was offered a place as a cancellation had come in.

I could remember being in Crumlin Road prison and hearing the voices of children nearby. Nobody seemed to know where it was coming from, but we found out it was St Malachy's College, which was situated over the high prison wall. As I lay on my back in my cell listening to the children's voices, up to my neck in the IRA, little did I know that nine years later I would be employed in that school as a Religious Education teacher. If I look out the window of my classroom today, I can clearly see the cell I served my time in.

I began to work on retreat teams with people I had met in Medjugorje, and I am very involved with the St Vincent de Paul charity. My religion helped me so much when I got out of prison and, through the sacraments, I was able to make the right choices. It helped me break the addiction and it was a real religion that I was experiencing, it was no longer a ritual religion. I always remembered the messages of Medjugorje and how Our Lady was calling for *Mir*, meaning peace. A group of friends and I got together and decided to get a peace petition together with signatures. It was at the height of the arms struggle but we got twenty-eight thousand signatures of young people throughout Ireland.

When I think about Medjugorje, I think about Jesus and how I found a loving Saviour whom I felt close to. I developed a love for the Mass, the Gospel and the word of God over there and really experienced the joy of forgiveness. I learned to deeply appreciate other people and, through my work with the St Vincent de Paul, I discovered a deep desire to help the poor. Through Medjugorje, I found a calling to evangelise and teach others about this living God, and I also developed a real love and special devotion to Our Lady. I also came to the realisation that I was, and always would be, a sinner who was loved.

4

Chris Rogers

United Kingdom

Chris Rogers is an award-winning investigative journalist and television presenter. He has worked with Sky News, ITV News *and the* BBC. *He first visited Medjugorje at the age of fifteen and struck up a friendship with the youngest of the visionaries, Jacov Colo. Chris had a personal experience on this trip and came home determined to be a priest. However, his life took a very different path and he made a successful career for himself in broadcast journalism. Fifteen years later, Chris returned to Medjugorje to write a feature for* The Times *newspaper. During this visit, Chris met with Jacov once again and they visited a place which had a profound impact on Chris' life and his career.*

This is Chris' testimony.

I was fifteen when I went on a school trip to Medjugorje. Throughout my childhood, my grandmother often brought the story of Lourdes and Fatima alive with her talent for catching your imagination. So when I learned of a school trip to a remote village where there are claims of Marian apparitions, I was desperate to go, out of curiosity more than anything else, but also to get a scoop. I arrived without a spiritual agenda; all I wanted was to interview the so-called visionaries. I was working as a voluntary reporter for a BBC youth radio programme. What I didn't know then was the impact that Medjugorje would have on my life, and not necessarily in a spiritual way.

As I got my story, I struck up a friendship with Jacov Colo, the youngest of the visionaries, who was ten when he and his friends first claimed to have seen the Virgin Mary. He was seventeen when I met him and he didn't speak much English, but we bonded over our shared interest in U2 and girls. The difference between us was that Colo could speak openly about his faith while I found talking about religion vaguely embarrassing. I'd been brought up to believe in God, and I did, but I didn't talk about it. Colo inspired me because he lived his faith in a way that I had thought impossible for anyone as trendy and as normal as he was.

On the third day of the trip, my classmates and I climbed up Podbrdo Hill, or the Hill of Apparitions as it's now known, to witness Ivan Ivankovic, Colo's neighbour, experience a vision. I sat on a rocky mound, and remember looking around at the thousands of praying, singing pilgrims and feeling distinctly conned. Suddenly there was silence. Ivankovic had fallen to his knees and was staring at the sky in what appeared to be a state of ecstasy. Stranger still, everyone else on the hill was staring at me. I was in the spot where Ivan claimed that his vision was appearing.

Out of respect – and embarrassment – I turned round, knelt and prayed. There was nothing. No heavenly lady, no supernatural lights, not even a hint of a vision. But as I prayed I began to feel a closeness to God and Our Lady that I had never felt before. I could feel tears of happiness streaming down my face. I was praying because this was what I wanted to do. At that moment my faith stopped being routine and became very real. I came back determined to become a priest.

However, that isn't what happened. The bishop told me, kindly but firmly, that while my experiences in Medjugorje were important, I did not have a vocation. So I focused on becoming a broadcast journalist instead. At twenty-one I married a beautiful South African, but the marriage broke down and at twenty-six, after I had walked out on her, the Catholic Church annulled the marriage on the grounds that we would not have married had she been British. This was perhaps true, but it did not erase the pain of a bitter divorce.

By then, all I had experienced in Medjugorje was a distant memory. I was reporting from disaster zones where I saw children dying and men blown apart, and my personal life felt disastrous too. By the time I turned thirty in 2004, I felt battered and numb, and my faith had become a private and lonely affair. I needed a spiritual reawakening, and that was when I decided to return to Medjugorje.

I arrived on a tourist coach full of British pilgrims, all about my age. But I was no ordinary pilgrim; I had funded the trip with a commission from *The Times* newspaper. The editor wanted me to write a personal account of how I felt Medjugorje had changed in the fifteen years since my first visit as a teenager. I would return with a very different story that would change the course of my life forever. I knew that the town had attracted twenty-five million visitors since 1981, some doubtlessly enticed by the apparitions that were said to happen at 6.40 p.m. each day. I knew that the visionaries had become international celebrities, and that they continue to be regarded with ambivalence by the Vatican, which has never acknowledged the apparitions as genuine. I knew, too, that although there was no fighting in Medjugorje during the Bosnian War, it was used as a UN base, and had lost many of its young men, who were conscripted. So I was surprised and disappointed at the commercialisation that had taken root.

My first impression was of entering a religious Costa del Sol. Souvenir shops selling kitsch statues of the Virgin and neon-lit restaurants crowd around the small church of St James. Yet once I began to walk around I found the calm and devotion of my fellow pilgrims infectious. At night I climbed the Hill of the Cross, a focal point for private prayer, and watched the sun rise. Perhaps it was the beauty that inspired me, but I began to feel a sense of peace.

Ivan Ivankovic invited me to join him during one of his apparitions. He sat me right beside him and winked, and placed my photographer on the other side of him, and winked at him. It was as if he was saying, 'I have nothing to hide, you can have front row seats.'

He looked more tubby and Americanised – spending half the year in the US with his American wife and children, and insists that wherever he is, his daily apparitions never cease. He invited me to join in a small prayer room with two priests and a prayer group. I watched as he claimed to experience another apparition, falling to his knees, his face relaxing and beaming. Again, I saw nothing, yet I felt the presence of something I can't explain – call it God, or something holy or spiritual, but to me, it felt as though someone had hugged me and said, 'Don't worry, stop looking so hard.' I felt humbled, saddened that I'd got so much wrong during the previous fifteen years. Fast cars, a nice house and a good career suddenly seemed insignificant. It was like falling in love – you don't know what it is but you know that it is real.

Later, Ivankovic told me that he had considered the priesthood and entered a seminary, but felt unwelcome because the Catholic Church does not recognise Medjugorje. He chose to leave and marry instead.

I watched Mirjana Dragicevic too, as she had her monthly apparition in front of coachloads of pilgrims. There were hundreds there, united through prayers and music – it felt like a religious Glastonbury, and reminded me of my experience fifteen years earlier. Whatever you think of the apparitions – and there is no scientific evidence to support them or disprove them – the atmosphere of hundreds of people singing and praying does mean that you don't feel like an outcast for having faith.

I wanted to get back in touch with Jacov Colo. He was initially wary – he has grown tired of journalists trying to disprove his claims – but, perhaps sensing that my purpose was personal, he invited me to his home where he lives with his wife and three children, and where he provides accommodation for pilgrims. He married, as I did, at twenty-one and I felt jealous of his happiness, which is clearly strengthened by the faith he and his wife share. He still talks of the apparitions with passion and I felt touched that someone who seemed so normal could have such a powerful spiritual dimension in his life.

Ultimately I found my renewed contact with Colo a more powerful influence than the apparitions. In just a few days I had found a friend with whom I could laugh, share a drink – and share a belief in God. Colo's contentment, and the ease with which he lives with his faith, inspired me.

You can spend too much time in Medjugorje looking to the apparitions for answers, and for proof that God exists. I found everything I was looking for within myself, but it was Medjugorje that gave me the space and calm to do so. My week was almost over and I was ready to file my copy to *The Times* and head home feeling much more positive about life. But a final visit to Jacov's house to say goodbye would send me home with a very different story.

As we sat in his garden sipping home-made lemonade, Jacov's three children captured his attention for a moment as they came screaming into the garden, chasing the family dogs. His mood suddenly changed, as if the children had prompted a disturbing memory. After a long pause, he asked if I and Matt Writtle, the photographer I was travelling with, would do him a favor: 'I want to show you something which has shocked me.'

He explained that he had discovered a neglected orphanage near Sarajevo, the capital city. Perhaps we might take some photos which he could show to pilgrims to help raise much-needed funds?

'If you are willing, I will take you there. The children desperately need help.'

I knew Jacov was orphaned himself, so if nothing else I felt it was worth the six hour round trip to get an extra insight into his unusual life for my *Times* article. But I was also keen to find out what exactly it was that he found so disturbing.

As we sped through the rugged mountain scenery, reminders of the terrible war were everywhere. Few of the villages we passed were untouched. Houses were peppered with bullet holes, some of them still without roofs. And as we got closer to Sarajevo the landscape became littered with completely bombed-out buildings. For the first time I was getting a true sense of the awful reality of the Bosnian War.

Jacov told us that the institution he was taking us to was full of children orphaned or abandoned during the war. I had never actually been to an orphanage and was unsure what to expect, but I began to fear that it wouldn't be good. As we entered the outskirts of Sarajevo, I noticed queues of families gathering outside what looked like an air-raid shelter, its pock-marked walls witness to ferocious fighting in the war.

'That's now a feeding centre for thousands of homeless families,' Jacov informed me. 'Little has changed in the ten years since the end of the war. Sarajevo is a city still scared and struggling to move on.'

We turned into a long drive strewn with rubbish. At the end of it was a bleak, grey building which could easily have been mistaken for another ruin. Half its roof was missing and the concrete walls had cracks so huge you could see through them.

Two tired-looking nurses and a doctor dressed in a tatty white coat were at the doorway to greet us. Jacov had clearly been here many times; they embraced him warmly.

The doctor reached out to shake my hand, introducing himself as Zihad Korjenic, the chief social worker. 'Are you prepared for this?' he asked gently.

'Prepared for what?' I wondered, casting Matt a glance.

At this point our interpreter, Brankcia Boras, a mother of three, shook her head and said to me, apologetically, 'I can't do this Chris. I'm going to stay outside.'

Dr Zihad gestured towards the doorway. 'Before you go inside I want you to know we are good people. We do everything we can for our patients. But it isn't much.'

As he opened the door, I was overwhelmed by the stench, a powerful, musty odour of urine and sweat. It was all I could do not to retch.

'You will get used to it, I promise,' Jacov whispered to me.

I walked down a long corridor, its bare walls stained yellow from tobacco smoke. It led to a dozen small rooms. I poked my head round the door of the first one, and couldn't believe what I saw. Lying across just three beds were fourteen children, aged from about eight to fifteen. They were tucked up next to several old, emaciated men and women. The sheets were stained with excrement and sweat, and though it was boiling outside, the windows were shut.

I was speechless. Eventually, I managed to ask Dr Zihad, 'Why are there adults here?'

'They came here as children around fifty years ago and have never left,' he answered. 'Their families have never come to see them since. They have nowhere to go.'

Each face, young or old, was emotionless. I smiled and waved hello, but there was no reaction. In the corner, a TV was showing some sort of game show. Applause and laughter echoed round the sparse room, but neither the children nor adults paid any attention. Some of them lay on their beds staring at the ceiling, seemingly unaware of anything else around them. Others, tied to cheap plastic chairs, rocked backwards and forwards.

'They rock to comfort themselves. We just don't have the staff to give them attention,' explained Dr Zihad. 'It's heartbreaking.'

I was utterly unprepared for suffering and neglect on this scale, and struggled to hold myself together. Dr Zihad reeled off a shopping list of resources the orphanage urgently required: 'We need the basics –

food, underwear, shoes and medicine – before we can even begin to think about specialist equipment. We want to separate the children from the adults but we do not have enough space. We need a new building, and then we can move the patients and give them proper therapy. All we can offer them right now is love – when we have time.'

At that moment, one of the children screamed out 'Mama!'. A nurse rushed into the room, scooped the child up and placed her on the floor, yanking down her trousers at the same time. Urine splashed onto the concrete floor all around her.

'The children always call me Mama,' explained the nurse. 'They never make it to the toilet – not that it works anyway – so I have to stop them peeing on the beds. This is the only way.'

I was witnessing the most unimaginable, undignified existence. As the staff themselves acknowledged, this was not an orphanage. It was a building full of dying rooms. And each room revealed more horrific suffering. Jacov took me into one area crammed with cots, containing not babies but teenagers tied to the rusting bars with pieces of cloth. All were staring at the blank walls in silence.

'These children were abandoned by their parents because they could not afford to take care of them. They are all severely physically and mentally disabled.'

I am no expert, but it seemed clear that most of the children's disabilities had been made worse by the years of subhuman treatment. I stroked the face of a ten-year-old called Mina and she smiled back. But a hug was impossible. A bandage had been wrapped around her waist pinning her arms behind her back. Her feet were tied to the end of the cot.

Another girl was sitting up in bed, with just her legs bound together. In the midst of this living hell, it was her story that finally caused me to break down. The nurse told me that for just a few minutes each day they untied her arms so she could read a postcard from her parents. The postcard had been delivered to the orphanage ten years earlier, the only one she had ever received.

I watched Jacov trying to get a smile out of the children, stroking their faces and hands and pulling silly faces. It struck me that, as an orphan himself, this was intensely personal for him; had his relatives not taken him in, he could easily have ended up in a place like this.

When my article appeared in *The Times*, the reaction was phenomenal. Many readers sent donations to a local charity, and conditions at the orphanage soon began to improve. Jacov phoned me in London to say they'd just taken delivery of a truckload of therapy equipment, and Dr Zihad even got his new building so he could at last separate children from adults.

Back in the ITV newsroom I felt reinvigorated. Not only was there the satisfaction of feeling 'job done', I now had my sense of direction. I would try to focus my future TV career on exposing injustice and human suffering around the world, especially where children were involved.

But it was all about to happen far more quickly than I could possibly have imagined. A call came through to the newsroom from a small human rights organisation called Mental Disability Rights International, based in Washington DC. Its director, Eric Rosenthal, had seen my article in *The Times* about the Sarajevo orphanage, and called to tell me that what I had uncovered was in his view just the tip of the iceberg.

'If you can pull it off, I suggest you head to Romania,' he advised me. 'People think the problems there are over, but they are simply covered up. It won't be easy and you'll have to go undercover, but multiply what you found in Sarajevo by about two hundred and you'll be close to the scale of the problem there.'

It was a phone call that would lead to a host of undercover investigations over the next three years. I would discover that more than a million children are being held in inhumane conditions across Europe. There would be death threats from gangsters, and acts of intimidation and slander from government ministers and secret police.

In 2006, armed with hidden cameras, I smuggled myself into the state-run orphanages of Romania, posing as an aid worker, and discovered the heartbreaking truth – that the conditions which had so shocked the world after the fall of communism in the early nineties had, in many cases, not improved. Children were still being abandoned: unloved, uncared for, even left to die. In their poverty, some families were prepared to sell their children illegally to wealthy westerners. The resulting films on ITV News and CNN sparked a global debate over the ban on international adoption from Romania, and led to more undercover trips. Gathering support from aid workers, politicians and finally a duchess and two princesses, I would expose the scandal of more than a million children held in inhumane conditions.

My investigations led to a European Union investigation and I was called to the chamber to give evidence. Romania was sanctioned and an independent EU committee was set up to oversee reform.

In 2008, Sarah, the Duchess of York, had been watching TV one evening when, by chance she caught one of my special reports on ITV News about the terrible conditions in Romanian orphanages. She was so deeply affected that she got in touch with me, offering whatever help she could in bringing the children's plight to the attention of the world. It was a phone call that would lead to a documentary television film with the Duchess and her daughters, Princesses Beatrice and Eugenie, going undercover with me to expose horrific conditions, not just in Romania, but another country with EU ambitions – Turkey. Both countries were furious that royalty had gone undercover in their institutions. Turkey tried to ban the film and extradite me and Sarah for trial. In a country where there is no freedom of press, secret filming is illegal. The British government called a press conference to try and calm diplomatic tensions. The global headlines were daunting.

The diplomatic storm over the documentary hovered for many more years. Today, Turkey is still investigating the possibility of the arrest of me, the Duchess of York, and key members of the production team for trespassing on orphanage territory and filming without permission. Feeble as the accusation seems, the Duchess and I find it very unsettling: Turkey has even involved the European police agency Interpol, and it is hard to be absolutely sure how far such an unprecedented case will go.

More than six million people tuned in to ITV to watch the two special editions of the *Tonight* programme. Millions more watched the documentary in other countries across the globe. Shortly after transmission, I asked Sarah if she ever regretted taking part in the film.

'There were days when I thought: "Ahhhh! What have I done?"' she admitted, 'But then I thought: "No, you have got to come out of a corner now, Sarah; you have got to be who you are meant to be, and stand up with courage for what you think is right." I sort of needed a kick up the backside to get back onto the public stage and be true to myself, without worrying too much about who I upset.'

Sarah quizzed me in return, 'What about you, what is your inspiration? Why so many investigations on the abandonment of children? Something must have driven you?'

'Well, I guess it is my job, but it was a story that didn't let go of me, rather than me not letting go of the story,' I told her. Then, for some reason, I went right back to the beginning of my journey, explaining how I came across the horrific orphanage in Sarajevo, while on assignment to report on Medjugorje, 'And one story on abandoned children simply led to another.'

Sarah's face suddenly lit up: 'Yes, wonderful place, Medjugorje.'

'You've heard of it?' I asked.

'Heard of it?' she laughed. 'I've been there! Whatever your faith, whatever your beliefs about that place, you cannot deny something special is happening there, be it spiritual or something else – Medjugorje inspires incredible journeys in people's lives. Maybe, just maybe, Chris, this was meant to be our journey.'

5

Méabh Carlin

IRELAND

Méabh was just nineteen years old when she was in a very serious hit-and-run accident while in Madrid in the summer of 2011, which left her wheelchair-bound. She visited Medjugorje the following year, although she didn't go to ask for a miracle, rather in thanksgiving for the gift of life. Over there, she felt God had a plan for her and she had some profound experiences both on Apparition Hill and at the Stations of the Cross. She returned to Medjugorje the following year with a group of young people for the Youth Festival, this time without a wheelchair.

This is Méabh's testimony.

The mystery of God's plan is something I often reflect upon. When we look at a tapestry being created, we see many threads being woven carefully together. The process can seem confusing and as we look closely, the work appears to be a rainbow of tangled knots. If we wait patiently for all of the threads to be used accordingly and look at the tapestry from a distance, we are able to see the beauty of the entire picture, and how each individual thread has a special part to play in the final product.

Thread by thread, God creates the tapestry of our lives. Sometimes we get glimpses of His beautiful creation, and with these little tasters come a deep sense of joy and contentment. We rest assured in the words of Mother Teresa when she said, 'You are exactly where you are meant to be.'

In the summer of 2012, after spending a week in the beautiful village of Medjugorje, it was clear that it had been carefully planned by God, and that I was indeed exactly where I was meant to be. I had been

55

involved in a very serious hit-and-run car accident while on pilgrimage in Madrid the previous summer, which had left me wheelchair-bound; a shock to my nineteen-year-old system, considering I had led a very active life as a ballet dancer. The night of my accident, as I lay on what I believed to be my deathbed, I remember what my final words were before losing consciousness. I began shouting the Hail Mary with every ounce of energy I had in my broken body. As I prayed the final words, 'now and at the hour of my death, Amen', I felt a deep sense of peace wash over my entire body. The storm within me calmed and I was ready to join God.

When children fall and hurt themselves, often the only form of miraculous consolation is that provided by their mother; the kiss that has the power to heal any wound. I find it most comforting to know that I called upon the nearest mother at hand, and was consoled in the way I needed to be during those traumatic moments. I promised that if I woke to see the light of day again that I would live every moment in thanksgiving to God for the gift of life I felt slipping through my fingers.

From that moment to now, I know Our Lady has been watching over me closely. Handing over my worries to her in prayer gave me the strength to accept the cross I had been given and provided me with peace and strength to endure many of the trials that the accident brought before me.

My journey to the town of Our Lady, Queen of Peace was especially poignant. I wasn't there to ask for a miracle, but to thank God and His mother for the strength they had given me. The miracle of Medjugorje for me at that time was the peace to be felt in the simple and humble little village sheltered by the beautiful, green surrounding mountains. As I looked at the tall mountains, I thought about God, my rock and my shield. It reminded me that I am just a pencil in the hand of God, the artist. That week I prayed that I could be used by Him in whatever way He had planned.

At times during my recovery I often struggled with the looks of pity I received from people as I wheeled passed them. Medjugorje was different – when people looked at me, they seemed to just see me and not the wheelchair. It was the first time I had been away from home after being discharged from hospital. Being away from the hustle and bustle of my usual routine of hospital appointments and physio-therapy sessions finally gave me an opportunity to be still. Life can be so noisy, and I often ask myself why we feel noise is necessary; playing music in the car, turning on the television for background noise, clapping after performances. It occurred to me that God speaks loudest in the silence of our hearts. It is difficult to hear His voice in a world so noise-orientated. In this simple, silent village I began to develop an understanding for the beautiful words of Psalm 46, 'Be still and know that I am God.'

During my week in Medjugorje, it became apparent that there were many knots to be untangled in my heart and that the trauma of my accident was very fresh. I remember wheeling around the Stations of the Cross. I had never taken time to really reflect upon the suffering Jesus endured. As I reflected on each station, I felt I could identify with Jesus in a small way. When he had his garments removed, my memory flashed back to the moment I was cut out of my dress on the street of Madrid in front of crowds of people. Jesus knew how exposed and embarrassed I felt. I then watched Jesus fall three times, but continue to pick up the heavy cross and walk forward in faith. It made me think of all the times I had tried to walk, and filled me with determination to continue to get up as He did, to 'walk by faith, not by sight' (2 Cor 5:7). The Stations of the Cross in Medjugorje lead to one of the most quiet and beautiful statues, the statue of the risen Christ. People wait patiently to touch this miraculous statue that weeps oil from the knees. No one can source where the oil is coming from.

Watching people faithfully line up to collect the precious oil fuelled my faith. The unity of man and God, which can be seen through holy people we encounter on our own faith journey, fills my heart with the mystery of God. As I looked at the face of the statue, I was moved by the painful expression on Jesus' face. I couldn't break eye contact with Him. He was broken, tired and weary. As I sat in my wheelchair, physically broken, I felt a powerful connection. For one of the first times since my accident I felt warm tears bouncing down my cheeks. I felt my heart being emptied of all the pain I hadn't allowed myself to feel. I stayed in that place and mourned the loss of my dancing, the ability to walk, my freedom and independence. I allowed myself to be honest about my fears for the future. It was in that special place that a miracle in my heart took place. I handed over all of my worries to Jesus and for every tear I shed, I felt a knot in my heart being untied.

I remember being carried by two men up one of the small mountains. No one asked the two men to do it, it was almost as if it was normal. I wasn't made to feel any different because I couldn't walk with the rest. In this little place of paradise it didn't matter who you were, what you looked like, whether you could walk, see or speak. Everyone was treated equally and their differences celebrated. It was like the garden of God, filled with His different flowers. Everyone in Medjugorje was able to open their beautiful petals towards His light and embrace themselves as His unique creations.

My week in Medjugorje was a week of healing. It planted a seed in my heart and I had a burning desire to bring other people to this still place. I prayed that God would use His little pencil to create something beautiful.

I never believed that the following summer I would return on my two feet with a group of fifty-five young people to participate in the Youth Festival. It was overwhelming to revisit all of the little places I had once wheeled. The feeling of the ground beneath my feet was heavenly. The first place I visited on that evening was the statue of the risen Christ. I thanked God for bringing me back in full health. I prayed that He would use me to bring that peace into any troubled heart that yearned for it.

The group of young people were all so different. They came to Medjugorje carrying their own intentions. We came as a music ministry, and much of the week we were united in song, and could be heard above the crowds. During the week we shared times of reflection; we climbed the mountains, attended daily Mass and prayed the rosary. Many of the young people weren't accustomed to praying a daily rosary. It is a long prayer, but when we are able to truly connect with each mystery, it becomes so special. People outside the Catholic faith often find it difficult to understand why we pray to Our Lady. I believe it's like picking the most perfect gift for a friend and trying to wrap it. But in my case, I always end up tearing the paper and getting sticky tape everywhere. So many times, my own mother has swooped in and saved the day by wrapping my present and adding her special motherly touch, tying a perfect bow and making my own attempt look perfect. In the same way, when we pray to Jesus and struggle to find words, Our Lady is able to come to our assistance, wrapping our prayers beautifully, exactly how she knows her son would like to receive them, and then present them on our behalf.

In our group, praying the rosary was something each person gradually began to enjoy more and more. A pair of rosary beads almost looks like a series of knots, one after the other eventually leading to Jesus on the cross. It became apparent, that with every bead a new knot in the heart of someone in our group was being untied.

During the week we had taken time to write our intentions on a large wooden cross. We planned on carrying the cross to the top of Cross Mountain, physically taking the weight of all of our burdens and heaviest struggles and leaving it at the top of the mountain. It was such an uplifting experience. The faith of the young people working together and helping each other with the weight of the cross was beautiful. Exactly how we should live our lives, loving God and our neighbour.

On the evening of my accident, a Jesuit priest placed a special wooden cross around my neck. It was something I felt had given me strength. The little wooden treasure had been with me during those lonely hours I spent in the intensive care unit and through many trials that followed. The same Jesuit priest had inspired me to pray to St Ignatius of Loyola, who had experienced a similar trauma in his life, which resulted in his beautiful conversion. I knew St Ignatius along with the other saints had carried me through my darkest moments, and as I stood at the top of Apparition Hill that week with my special cross around my neck, I thanked God for the gift it was to be so close to heaven.

I remained on the mountain while others walked down. I closed my eyes and entered into a beautiful time of prayer. All I could hear was the wind blowing around me. My prayer was interrupted by the sound of a crowd of people walking. I opened my eyes to see four men carrying a girl on a stretcher. I was brought back to the previous year when I had been in that girl's position. I didn't like to invade her privacy, but I couldn't help but watch as she was placed at the foot of the statue of Our Lady. There was another lady standing behind her. I watched the girl look up at Our Lady and almost like a volcano erupting she began to cry uncontrollably. I cried with her, and prayed that she would receive healing in exchange for her tears. As I continued to pray for this girl I didn't even know, I felt a voice in my heart telling me I had to give her my special cross. It had served me well.

I wiped away my tears and approached the girl. I didn't know if she might reject it or feel patronised but I walked up to her, put my hand onto her shoulder and pressed the wooden cross into her palm. As I turned to walk away I heard someone call after me in Spanish. It was the girl's mother. She embraced me and began crying in my arms before asking me what my name was in Spanish. I replied saying the only thing I had ever known in Spanish, 'Me llamo Méabh.' I let go of her hand and made my way down apparition hill. I couldn't see where my feet were going for the constant supply of water blurring my vision. The last time I had remembered saying 'Me llamo Méabh' was the night of my accident as I was crowded with panicked doctors and nurses. Those three chilling words were the only thing that bridged the gap between the Spanish staff and me. I was overwhelmed and not sure how I felt.

Later that evening we had a time of prayer and reflection with the priest leading our group. He began by telling us that it was the feast day of St Ignatius of Loyola. It was then that I knew St Ignatius had been the one to keep me on the mountain and had planted the idea in my heart of giving my little Jesuit cross away. It was such a simple act but I will never be able to forget the face of the girl when I presented it to her. It made me think of the words of Mother Teresa, 'We cannot all do great things, only little things with great love.' It was such a small act, but there was so much love exchanged in that brief encounter, enough to sustain me for a lifetime.

As the youth week came to a climactic close, it was amazing to see the change in our group. It was like watching ice melt into water. I thought about how ice cubes are all carefully frozen into identical moulds, they are often difficult to get out, cold and solid. I thought about the young people in our group and the struggle of many young people striving to find their place, and in some cases doing everything to fit into the moulds set by society, the media and celebrities. For that week in Medjugorje, every young person was able to gently allow God to come into their hearts. The fire of faith was able to melt away their insecurities and by the end of the week we were united as one cup of God's love and joy.

Medjugorje for me is a place of beauty, stillness and above all else peace. It is a place where many fires for God are reignited, a place where God's presence can be felt in the scenery, the prayerful sanctuaries and in the beautiful people that He uses to be His instruments. I pray that God will use me as His instrument to bring other people to Medjugorje, to witness the song of His peace that comes from His mother. My experiences in that beautiful village are difficult to describe and impossible to express; only God knows, as He continues to add to the tapestry of my life.

6

Bernard Ellis

UNITED KINGDOM

Bernard Ellis grew up in an Orthodox Jewish family. From a young age, he admits to being told that Catholics were demonic people who 'ate flesh' and 'drank blood'. His wife heard about the apparitions in Medjugorje and convinced him to take her there. Bernard admits to being the only person present during an apparition who didn't kneel, as he believed it was wrong to kneel before a 'graven image'. He returned to Medjugorje a few more times and became known as the 'Jewish Catholic' who kept coming to Medjugorje. He has now converted to Catholicism.

This is Bernard's testimony.

I was brought up in an Orthodox Jewish family in North London. In the area where I lived, there was a big division between Catholics and Jews and there was a lot of animosity between them. The Jewish people thought the Catholics were demonic because they 'ate flesh' and 'drank blood' and because they prayed to a spirit and worshipped a 'woman god'. There was a lot of tension between the two groups and even my father and my mother, having come from Poland and Russia, were very anti-Catholic. They had to leave their countries of birth because of anti-Semitism, mostly at the hands of Catholic people. Unfortunately, some of my relatives were killed in the gas chambers at Auschwitz, and this only heightened the animosity my parents felt towards Catholics.

I fell in love with a Catholic girl, who at the time was more of a 'Sunday Catholic'. I was in my early twenties at this time, and although I believed in God, I didn't follow any religion. We got married and were very happy together. We had two girls, twin boys and then another little girl. One day, my wife was cleaning our local church in Caterham along with another woman, when the other woman turned to my wife and asked her if she had heard that the Blessed Virgin was appearing to six children in Yugoslavia. My wife was intrigued and asked the woman to tell her more, however, the woman declined and said she wouldn't tell her because it wasn't true. She advised her not to get involved in it but my wife was very interested in what might have been happening there. She went to Westminster Cathedral one day and picked up a pamphlet by a man called Peter Batty who was one of the first people in England to promote what was happening in Medjugorje. She read the pamphlet and immediately believed it.

A short while later, my wife asked me to take her to Medjugorje. She said that we could have a holiday in Yugoslavia and just visit Medjugorje for two or three days. I told her that it would be wrong of her to expect me to go to this Catholic shrine, where there would be people lying on the floor, praying, and drinking watery soup. I told her it was no place for a Jewish man to go. My wife told me that if I really loved her, I would take her there. I replied by saying that if she really loved me, then she wouldn't want me to go there. So, we didn't go.

About a year later, my wife turned to me again and said, 'Let's go on a holiday to Dubrovnik.' I asked her why she wanted to go to this communist country and she told me about this lovely hotel that was on the beach and how the children would love it. I knew deep down inside that it wasn't really the hotel in Dubrovnik that attracted her but that she really wanted to go to Medjugorje. I told her what I thought and she admitted that I was right. She promised me we would just go to visit Medjugorje for two days out of the two week holiday and so I eventually agreed.

When we arrived on our holiday to Dubrovnik, we met some people in the hotel who also had young children, and they offered to mind our children while we visited Medjugorje. We asked at the reception of the hotel, how to get there. They told us that it was a long way to go and said that it was only a field, and, if we wanted to go to a field to pray, there were plenty of fields around Dubrovnik. This was in 1983 and although it was difficult to get there, we decided to hire a car. We got some maps and asked a lot of people for directions and eventually we arrived in the village.

We climbed Podbrdo and Krizevac and although there were very few English speaking people there, Fr Tomislav Pervan, who was the parish priest at the time, did speak English. We asked him if he had a video of what was happening here. He told us that he had but that he wouldn't show it to just two people and would need at least six. We found three more people and went back to the priest and he showed us the video. We were intrigued and my wife asked if we could stay for the evening Mass, as she wanted to be near to where the apparition was taking place. At this time, the apparitions took place in a room beside the altar. There were lots of people queuing up outside the presbytery, as they wanted to be present too.

A lady called Anita Curtis was helping Fr Pervan and she knew who I was and that I was Jewish. She asked the priest to let me into the apparition room because I was Jewish and she said that the Blessed Mother would be pleased to see me. I thought this was complete nonsense, because if the Blessed Mother was coming through time and space, then it wouldn't matter if I was on the inside or the outside of the wall. There were lots of people begging to get into the room; I saw a woman with a disabled child and she was crying and begging to go in, because she thought that if she went in then her child would be cured. I said to Fr Pervan, 'Let this woman go in and I will stay outside.' At that, he grabbed the woman with the child, grabbed me as well and then pushed all of us in.

We went into the room and I remember it was very hot as it was August. There was no air conditioning and the room was full of people standing shoulder-to-shoulder without an inch to spare. The visionaries came in and started praying and I remember there was a very poorly painted statue of Our Lady, which reminded me of Snow White. Suddenly, the visionaries knelt and looked up at the ceiling and as they were looking up, everybody in the room knelt down. I was the only one left standing. Jewish people don't kneel because in the Torah it says, 'You shall not worship a graven image.' To me, the statue was a graven image and I didn't want to kneel before it.

We were so tightly packed that as everyone went down to kneel, I was forced down with them. I remember feeling a knee in the back of my heel, another knee on my foot and someone was pushing me in my back and it was the most uncomfortable experience. I looked really hard at the ceiling and couldn't see anything at all but I kept looking and thinking about how uncomfortable people were. Suddenly, everyone stood up and the apparition had ended. We were ushered across the altar, out the side door and into the courtyard.

I saw my wife standing there with tears streaming down her face. I asked her why she was crying and she told me that she was just so happy and that I would never understand what a great privilege I just had. The previous Christmas, I had given her a set of hand-made, solid gold rosary beads. I noticed that she never really used the gold beads, just an ordinary wooden set and felt that maybe she thought they were too ostentatious. She had brought the gold beads to Medjugorje to get blessed and while we were in the courtyard, she asked me if she could give the gold rosary beads to the parish as a gift. I remember thinking, 'I wonder does she know just how much they cost?' I told her they were a gift to her and she should do with them whatever she liked.

She took the beads and gave them to Fr Pervan, who said he would put them in the parish archives. I often wondered what had happened to those beads so, years later, I asked him if he still had the beads. He told me that they were still in the archives and that one day they would open a museum and tell people that these beads were given to the parish by the wife of the Jewish Catholic.

About a year after this first trip, my wife asked me if we could go again to Medjugorje. Although I didn't believe that anything was happening there, I still thought that the village was a very peaceful place and the people very welcoming and kind. The Franciscans were particularly friendly to me, as I was a bit of a novelty – the Jewish man who didn't believe. So, the next year we went back to Medjugorje.

We heard that there was going to be an apparition at the top of Cross Mountain by Marija Pavlovic. My wife wanted to go, so we left very early and climbed the mountain. There were only a few people there when we arrived and so we sat down at the foot of the cross. My wife began telling me all the reasons why we should accept Christ as the Saviour and as the Messiah. For every good reason she gave, I had an equally good reason why He wasn't the Messiah and I told her I would never believe in Him.

Eventually darkness fell and we saw a choir coming up the mountain with lanterns. It was Marija and her prayer group. By this time, thousands had gathered and the crowd parted as she arrived. Marija came up to where we were sitting at the foot of the cross and she stood by my side. She looked up to the sky, started to pray and then fell on her knees again. A man from the prayer group turned to me and asked me if I spoke English. I told him yes, and he told me to tell everyone to kneel, to pray, and not to take any photographs. I turned around and in a loud voice said, 'Everybody kneel and don't take photographs, the Mother of God is appearing to Marija.' At that, they all knelt and only I was left standing. I felt embarrassed, as it was me who had told them to kneel, and so I knelt with them.

I looked up and although I didn't see anything, I remember thinking that the stones on the mountain were very sharp and that Catholics must have special knees to endure all this kneeling! As I was having these thoughts, which were not exactly holy, I felt a drop of rain on my head and I thought that it might pour rain any minute. I knew that the mountain would become slippery and dangerous and wanted to get down before the rain came. When the apparition ended, Marija gave the message to the people in Croatian and then it was translated into different languages. She said that the Blessed Mother appeared on a cloud and she spoke about bad things that were going to happen. As the Blessed Mother spoke about these things, a tear dropped down from her eye and landed on the cloud. I felt that I must have been kneeling just under that cloud. The rain never came, so I felt that maybe that teardrop fell on me. I dismissed it immediately, as I thought it was so unlikely.

We went back to the guest house we were staying in and there was a priest there called Fr Robert Cox. I told him what had happened and asked him what he thought it meant. He told me I was being called to Baptism. I didn't know what he meant and left it at that – I still didn't believe what was happening there in Medjugorje.

About two years later, we visited Medjugorje again. I was becoming quite well known as the Jewish man who kept coming to Medjugorje and I became quite friendly with Marija. One day, she invited me to be present during an apparition in her house. It was on the first floor and about sixty people turned up. They began to pray the rosary and then they all knelt when the apparition began. I stood at the back of the room and didn't kneel. I was looking at all these devout people praying with their eyes closed and hands raised up and I remember thinking that I was in a room with sixty people who believed and that I was the only man standing at the back who didn't believe. I said to myself that if the Blessed Mother is really appearing to Marija, then please give me a sign.

When the apparition ended, Marija got up and she spoke to a Croatian interpreter, who in turn spoke in English. He told us that the Blessed Mother had appeared and that she had spread her arms over those assembled, prayed for the sick, for all of us present and for our families. At the end, we were told that the Blessed Mother prayed with Marija and over all of us present in her native tongue, which was Hebrew Aramaic. I had asked for a sign and wondered if this was it. It was a powerful sign but I still didn't believe it was happening.

A year later, we went to hear Fr Jozo talk. He spoke well and I was impressed. As people started to leave, others began to line up because they wanted Fr Jozo to pray over them. I turned to my wife and told her that I would like Fr Jozo to pray over me so that the truth would be revealed to me. The feeling I had was very strong and so we waited in the line with the others. We were almost the last ones to go up to him and I spoke to his interpreter. I said, 'Could you ask Fr Jozo to pray over me, and tell him that I am Jewish. Can you tell him that I want God to reveal to me the truth?' He put one hand on my head and one on my heart and began to pray in Croatian. My heart began to pound very fast. I thought it would burst out of my shirt. My wife told me it was another sign and said I was too stubborn to believe in anything. I still didn't believe – I suppose Jewish people are stiff-necked, and can't be convinced too easily.

I had become quite friendly with Fr Slavko and he was interested in me, a Jewish man who kept coming to Medjugorje. Fr Slavko was speaking at a Charismatic meeting in Walsingham and we went there to listen. I still had no intention of changing my religion. When we got there, people were getting confession. When they did this, they were given a candle and this symbolised that they were coming from the darkness into the light. They were singing and dancing because their sins had been forgiven and they felt relieved and free. Fr Slavko came onto the altar to prepare for Adoration and stood quietly for ten minutes until people became silent. I had the opportunity to go to

Adoration many times before but I had never gone because the Jewish tradition forbade me to. To me, the monstrance was just a graven image with a wafer of bread in it.

For some reason, I stayed. I saw all the people kneel down and stare at the monstrance. I suddenly felt and sensed a presence staring back at them. As I felt this presence, I had a flashback of the three times I was given a sign in Medjugorje. I knelt down and instantly accepted the true presence of Jesus in the Eucharist. When I went home, I told my wife that I wanted to become a Catholic. Becoming a Catholic meant that I would receive the Eucharist, the body and blood of Christ, that would come to nourish me and to help me. There was also the sacrament of reconciliation and I felt that all the things I had done wrong, would be forgiven. If I became baptised, all my sins would be washed away. I went to my parish priest and told him I wanted to become Catholic. He was very pleased and he asked me why I was converting. I told him it was difficult to describe but that I was given the gift of knowing that Jesus was truly present in the Eucharist.

I became a Catholic a year later. I was baptised and had my first Holy Communion on Easter Thursday, the day of the Last Supper. It was the 13th of April, which was also my birthday and I felt it was a gift from Our Lady because I had been born again on my birthday. After that, I became a regular churchgoer and I am so grateful to God that this has been my experience.

What does Medjugorje mean to me?

Medjugorje was the real beginning of my conversion. I had three experiences in the village, and at that moment when I was given the gift of feeling the presence of God in the Eucharist, I knew Medjugorje was instrumental in opening my heart and my mind to the possibility of becoming a Catholic. I believe the three experiences were supernatural and that they led me to open my heart to accept Jesus in the Eucharist.

7

Lee Marshall

UNITED KINGDOM

Lee Marshall had a prosperous career as Financial Director of a large company in the UK. He had everything in terms of money, wealth and possessions. However, when he went home at the weekend, he found emptiness inside and deep down knew he wasn't really happy. His parents had been to Medjugorje and he noticed a change in them. Lee decided to go on pilgrimage to the village for the New Year of 2006. Whilst there, he had three experiences which had a great impact on his life and Lee felt God was calling him to the priesthood. He spent the next six years in a seminary in the UK and was ordained a priest in the summer of 2013.

This is Lee's testimony.

I came to Medjugorje for the first time on New Year's of 2006. It was a time in my life when everything seemed to be going really well for me in terms of my career. My whole adult life had been geared towards becoming successful in my job and earning as much money as I could. I took on this status of power and of being esteemed along with all the trappings of the world. At twenty-eight years of age, I was promoted to finance director of the company I was working for. I was a chartered accountant and the company had offices in Hong Kong and London. It was a fantastic job to get at such a young age. Everything seemed to have just fallen into my lap, but I was becoming trapped in a lifestyle of wealth and possessions.

Every weekend, when work was over and I had to face myself, I felt empty; my life lacked meaning and I was often downcast. I didn't feel any value or worth in what I was doing or where I was going. Around this time, my parents visited Medjugorje and I noticed a change in them. They never preached about their experience and yet they bore witness to it through their lifestyle. I could see a change in them and although we were brought up Catholics, their faith had now taken on a new power and a new meaning. It had become very important to them and I remember thinking that there was something very attractive about this.

In 2005, they invited me to come to Medjugorje with them and I said yes. For some reason, as the date got closer, I changed my mind and said no. I decided to go on holiday to Egypt instead. My mum had told me that you go to Medjugorje because Our Lady invites you and I remember feeling that I had turned the Blessed Mother down, that I had said 'no' to Mary.

Shortly after, I was in work and I got onto my computer and decided to book a trip to Medjugorje for New Year's. I thought I was being clever, as I wouldn't have to tell anyone in the office that I was going on pilgrimage because they would all be off work at this time.

I arrived in Medjugorje and I had the most incredible experience. As I was on the bus coming into the village, I prayed to Mary, telling her that there was only one thing I wanted. I wanted to open my heart to Jesus but felt I couldn't do it and I asked her to help me. In the job I was doing, I felt that my heart had become hard, as my work was often confrontational and I had become quite aggressive in my character. I had put on a mask which showed I was this strong, powerful, executive character. I found it difficult to relate to people or to know how to behave in other people's company.

I went to Holy Mass on New Year's Eve in St James' Church and I discovered for the first time that Mass was a celebration. I had regularly gone to Mass but it was always out of obligation and it was something that I never really connected with. But here in Medjugorje, it was a joyful experience and there were plenty of young people there and I found this quite moving.

The following night I was present during an apparition on the hill which I thought was incredible. The prayer and grace were overwhelming and I had a realisation in my heart that Mary was amongst us and that God exists and was here through Our Lady. I felt we were connected to heaven and that it was all real and very powerful. The following morning, I was present at one of Mirjana's apparitions, which took place in the Cenacolo community. To see the joy in her face as she saw Our Lady left no doubt in my mind that this was real. These three events had happened in quick succession. I was left almost floating, full of peace and joy, but it was a joy and peace that I had never experienced before. It was something that could only come from heaven. I was talking openly to people, was happy in my group and I could relate to people. I had really come out of my shell and I had left all that aggression behind. I was really discovering who I was.

This feeling continued for a few days and towards the end of my pilgrimage, I decided to buy a painting of the crucified face of Christ. I immediately realised that I had bought it for very superficial reasons. I bought it because I thought the colours would look good on my lounge wall. As I realised how shallow I had been, all the peace and joy I had received seemed to just leave me. I felt anxiety come back into my heart and I was back to where I was at the beginning of the pilgrimage. Everything had gone and I felt gutted. I wanted to get rid of the painting and get the joy back. For the rest of the day, I was in a daze. That evening, it was raining and dark and I decided to go for a walk.

I walked past the confessionals in the grounds of St James and I decided to join the queue. As I was queuing up, I felt a sudden awakening within me and it was like a light had been switched on. I realised that the source of my anxiety wasn't really to do with the painting at all, but with the fact that deep down I knew God wanted me to become a priest and I had always known this without ever acknowledging it. I thought the idea was crazy – I mean, why would I want to become a priest? I was anxious and fearful about this idea and so I planned on getting rid of it all in my confession. I thought I could leave it all there and get on with my life. I thought, 'Why would I want to give up my career, the money, the lifestyle, and the opportunity of getting married and having a family?' It seemed that God was offering so little and yet He wanted me to give up so much. I wasn't prepared to do that.

For some reason I was sure the priest hearing my confession would agree with me and so I was amazed to discover that in spite of my career and plans for the future, God might in fact have a better plan for me. It was a real moment of conversion because for the first time in my life I became aware of God's will and that he had a plan for me which might be different to my own. However, I was stunned by this new revelation, within a matter of minutes, my whole life, all my plans and desires, had been turned upside down. Within ten minutes of leaving the confessional I managed to dismiss the whole idea as madness and I decided I would just get on with the rest of my life.

I tried to do this. I left Medjugorje and went back to work. I can remember sitting at my desk and thinking that I couldn't do my job any more. In the past, I had enjoyed flying out to Hong Kong and loved the whole lifestyle but there was nothing in it for me any more. I felt that the only way I could cope at work was to have another pilgrimage to Medjugorje to look forward to, so I returned to the village four months later around Easter time. I was also fortunate enough to return the following September and New Year's. In all, I visited Medjugorje four times in that first year.

All throughout that year, I was trying to discern if God really wanted me to become a priest and whether I could be a priest. I felt like a swinging pendulum. One day I wanted it and the next day it seemed like the worst idea in the world. Eventually I became so frustrated that I decided to give the idea up and not to think about it further. Through the grace of God, all thoughts of the priesthood left me and for a while I felt content at work. However, when I returned to Medjugorje, one year after my initial pilgrimage, I felt an immediate, overwhelming desire to be a priest. After much prayer, I decided during that pilgrimage that I should go for it. God's initial call and my 'yes' to His will, all came through Our Lady at Medjugorje within the space of a year.

The only thing left for me to do was to tell everyone at work. First, I had to tell them that I was a Catholic and, by the way, I'm going to be a priest! I was dreading the moment – I mean, how do you just come out and say that? As the day got closer, I began to get really nervous. I knew that if I wanted to enter the seminary the following September, then I couldn't put it off any longer. The chairman of the company was a strong character and I wondered how he would take the news. However, when I told him, he just gave me a big hug. I told all the other directors and I was amazed at the supportive responses I received from them. I knew that I had to tell the rest of the three hundred and fifty employees, so I sent an email at 5 p.m. on Friday evening, hoping they would all be gone home for the weekend. However within minutes, I began to receive responses and all of them were beautiful and positive. In total, I received over one hundred emails of support.

Seven years ago, I sold my house, left my career, and I entered the seminary in September 2007. These last seven years have been the happiest of my life. To be in an environment of prayer, faith and discovering God's will every day has been such a blessing for me. I am on the threshold of a wonderful gift which God wishes to give to me. Our Lady loves us just as we are, but she also loves us because she sees who we can be. Eight years ago, when I first came here, Mary loved me just the way I was, but she loved me too much to leave me that way, because she also saw the person that God created me to be. The last eight years have been an incredible journey of self-discovery and I have Our Lady to thank for all the graces I have received through her motherly intercession and for all that God will do through me as a priest of Jesus Christ.

8

Carmen Dobbie

New Zealand

Carmen Dobbie first heard about Medjugorje back in the 1980s when her mother went to a talk. Although her mother asked her to accompany her to the village some years later, Carmen was reluctant, and was happy when her mother was unable to travel. However, over the next few days, Carmen felt a strong desire to visit Medjugorje on her own.

This is Carmen's testimony.

My name is Carmen and I live in New Zealand. I am one of three siblings raised in the Catholic faith by one very strong and courageous mother who, in adversity, stepped up to the challenge that God put in her way.

I first heard of Medjugorje in the late eighties, after my mother had attended a talk presented by an Australian called Leon Le Grand. He spoke of his conversion that took place after visiting this village where Our Lady had been appearing to a small group of children.

I can recall very clearly that my mother was convinced that what this man had spoken about was authentic to her. This was really saying something, as she was not someone that was easily duped. I didn't really have an opinion either way but felt happy for my mother, who had experienced great suffering in her life and it was clear that her faith was her rock.

In 2001, my mother expressed an interest in travelling to Medjugorje and asked me if I would accompany her there. Mum had recently had a brain tumour removed and there were obvious changes to her personality, which I could see would not make for an easy trip at all.

My reply to the invitation was 'yes', however deep down I thought the chances would be fairly remote, as mum was not a traveller at heart. Although she had enquired about seats, she had not put a deposit down. As the deadline for this particular trip approached, it became clear that mum would not be well enough to go. 'Thank goodness,' I said to myself with a sigh of relief, 'for one minute there I thought I was going to have to fly to the other side of the world to a place in the middle of nowhere!'

However, as the following week progressed, I experienced an overwhelming desire that I needed to go to Medjugorje myself. I could not rationalise why this was happening and for almost three days and nights, I was totally consumed with finding a pilgrimage that I could book which would get me to Medjugorje.

This, at the time, was crazy. I had a mother who was unwell and not settling into a rest home, three young children, a non-Catholic husband who was probably going to think I was mad, and virtually no holidays available with my workplace.

Eventually I booked a seat on a pilgrimage run by Kathryn O'Connor and that was to be a trip I will never forget, in more ways than one.

This, for me, was the start of a truly amazing journey of faith. What I recall as being the most significant thing was of actually being able to feel the tenderness of God's love for me during the exposition of the Blessed Sacrament. I had never experienced anything like this before and I felt so loved and precious. I would have to say that on this pilgrimage I also experienced a true sense of peace and confession in a way that I had never had before. While saying my penance next to the statue of the risen Christ, I experienced the miracle of the sun. I could not comprehend how this could be, as the sun appeared to be pulsating in different colours and constantly changing position in the sky. I put it down to jet lag, however I know deep down that what I experienced was for me and maybe a gift to say thank you for accepting an invitation to come.

Upon my return to New Zealand, staff who cared for my mother remarked on how calm she had become and she remained this way up until she died two years later. Since my first pilgrimage to Medjugorje, I have developed a very deep love for Our Lady and I pray the rosary as often as I can.

I have had several soul destroying events since this initial trip, including a divorce, and the diagnosis of a progressive eye disease that has now left me legally blind. I have returned to Medjugorje four times. Three of my children accompanied me on one trip and plan to return.

What I have experienced as a result of my trips to this Bosnian village, I can't entirely explain, however, I am convinced that one day I will understand. I do not fear for the future now and try very hard to live each day as it comes, as I know that I have Mary and her son at my side, guiding me.

What does Medjugorje mean to me?

Medjugorje for me is my sense of hope. It is my peaceful haven that really is heaven on earth. The fruits that I have experienced and continue to experience are proof to me that Mary's messages definitely are real and for our times. I have read that Mary invites us personally to go to Medjugorje. Little did I know that when my mother asked me to accompany her it was part of a much wider plan.

9

Alan Kavanagh

IRELAND

Alan Kavanagh was only seventeen years of age when he dived into the sea one summer's day in his hometown of Dublin and subsequently broke his neck. This left him paralysed from the neck down. After refusing to feel sorry for himself, Alan completed his studies and went on to set up a very successful business. Having visited his sister one day and hearing of her experience in Medjugorje, he decided to travel out there that summer. Over there, he learned how to pray the rosary and asked God to give him some guidance as to what he wanted him to do in this life. He eventually sold off his business and began concentrating on his faith.

This is Alan's testimony.

When I was a young lad, I was a bit of a wild fellow. I was always getting into trouble, skipping school and causing havoc for the family. As kids, we were sent to Newbridge College, a boarding school. To me, it was a little more like a jail than a school, and I never liked it much. However, as time went on, we all got settled in a bit more. In the summer of 1976, I was in fifth year of school and I came home for the summer. There was a heatwave that year and we all went down to the Bull Wall, which is a beach down in Clontarf, in Dublin. There was a diving board on the beach and it was a beautiful, sunny, August day, with lots of people around. I dived in, but in such a way that I hit the bottom of the sand and broke my neck. I have been paralysed from the neck down ever since.

I had a lot of time, lying in bed in hospital, to think about what the heck life was all about in the first place. What was I supposed to do with my life now? In the early days, we all thought that I might get better but that hope very soon evaporated into reality. No one got better in the hospital that I was in and therefore it was unlikely that I was going to be any different. The choice was given to me in my mind – well, what are you going to do now Alan? Lie back and feel sorry for yourself or get on with life? I wasn't interested with lying around doing nothing, so I decided to go back to school and finish my Leaving Certificate Exams. I went to Ballymun Comprehensive School and finished out my studies there. I passed all my exams and then stayed at home for a few months before I began to look for work. I applied for jobs that the government organised for people who are disabled. When I didn't get any of them, I decided to start my own business.

My brother and I set up our own business, selling pressure washers and car washers and we continued with the business for eighteen years. I was very happy and thoroughly enjoyed it and we both made a great success of it. We made a few bob and things were going great.

I had been going to Mass regularly and I enjoyed going as it always made me feel better. I never had any great faith, as such, but my Dad would march us up to Mass every Sunday when we were kids. We were always late but whatever that did for us as children, it left us with a great liking for the Mass and most of us kept the tradition going as we got older.

One day, I went to visit my sister in Bettystown with my girlfriend, who is now my wife. While we were there, my sister began talking about Medjugorje. She had gone on holiday to Croatia with her husband and they hadn't been far from Medjugorje. My sister had heard about the alleged apparitions on the news and elsewhere and she wanted to go and visit the village but her husband didn't want to go with her. She met a couple who had just spent a week in Medjugorje and they were now having a holiday by the beach for their second week. They told my sister all about their experiences and what was happening there. My sister and the couple then decided to hatch a plan to go back to the village for a day. My sister went in the car with the couple and my brother-in-law stayed on the beach, as he didn't have much time for religion. However, he did promise to drive to Medjugorje to pick up my sister that evening.

When he drove up, he was very frustrated trying to find her but eventually spotted her standing outside Vicka's house. As he saw her, for some reason he was drawn out of the car and towards a woman who was coming down the stairs of the house. The woman turned out to be Vicka. Immediately, Vicka began to pray over him and from then on, his life changed. Something had happened to him. He changed from being a person who had absolutely zero interest in faith or the Church and from having been a difficult husband, to a person who fell in love with God and Medjugorje and who became a wonderful, loving, caring husband.

As my sister was telling me this story, it really struck a chord with me and my girlfriend and we decided to go to Medjugorje that summer and see for ourselves what it was all about.

While we were in Medjugorje, we met Nancy and Patrick Latta, through my sister and her husband, who had befriended them. Fr Jozo was giving one of his talks and Nancy was doing the translation for him and so they invited us along. While we were in the car they said to us, 'We are going to teach you how to say the rosary.' I hadn't prayed the rosary since I was very small. If ever I did, it was only once or twice when my Dad decided he wanted us to pray it. As kids, we would swing the rosary beads around and have a bit of fun. I didn't really have a clue what the rosary was about or why it was said.

Patrick and Nancy started to pray the rosary and so we joined in with them. We said a decade each and funnily enough from that day to this, I have always prayed the rosary. I pray it every single day and I have a bit of an addiction with it. I can't actually miss saying it anymore.

We had a wonderful experience with Fr Jozo and he prayed over us while we were there. It was so special and I can only describe the feeling I got from it as being on a huge high. It was a wonderful, joyous, happy feeling which I hadn't had in a long time. I had a similar feeling when I went to Lourdes at the age of eighteen, just a year after I broke my neck. People had raised money and sent me to Lourdes with my brother and a friend of ours. However in Medjugorje, I felt like I was being taught the prayers and what I should do, and how to continue with it when I got home.

This visit to Medjugorje was a different experience for me. It was during the time when all the abuse scandals were coming out in Ireland. The Brendan Smyth scandal was huge at the time and I remember thinking to myself, how could the Church and the bishops keep moving these abusers around like they did? How could they possibly keep aiding and abetting them? This all had a big impact on me and I stopped going to church. This was about three months before my sister spoke to me about Medjugorje and it was really causing me a great dilemma inside. The truth was that I didn't feel good about not going to Mass and for those few months, I started to look at other faiths. I looked at the Muslim, Hindu and Buddhist faiths and started reading about them; I just thought that this Catholic faith couldn't be the one true faith with all this going on.

I remember praying to God that He would give me some guidance as to what exactly he wanted from me in this life because I was getting very confused. When I went to Medjugorje and went to Fr Jozo's talk, he gave us a picture of Our Lady with five instructions on the back. I remember immediately knowing in my heart that this was God saying to me, 'Here is your set on instructions that you were looking for.' The instructions were: prayer (the rosary), fasting on Wednesdays and Fridays, monthly confession, Holy Mass on Sunday, and to read Scripture daily. I remember thinking, 'My God, that is really something to ask of me.' I wasn't sure I would be able to do all that. Nevertheless, I decided to have a go anyway. With the exception of about three or four months recently, I have kept to the instructions from the day I received them.

By doing all this, I have found the most incredible, spiritual life, which is simply out-of-this-world. I have found a whole new meaning to life and to my existence and that gives me great joy and a feeling of great happiness inside. Everything we do, when it is united with Jesus and Our Lady and our family in heaven, has great meaning and great purpose. I find that if you are operating within the instruction and rules that they are giving you, your life becomes a happy one, even when things are difficult. When it is difficult, it puts meaning on everything.

My visits to Medjugorje have changed my life completely. Although I loved my business, after I got into my faith a bit more, I knew that chasing money was not what I wanted to do, and it wasn't giving me any satisfaction anyway. The things I was buying with the money I made from the business weren't really doing anything for me. The more things I got, the more I wanted and the less they meant to me. After a while, I became bored with it. What was I accumulating all this stuff for?

I decided in my mind that I wanted to get out of the business, but that wasn't going to be easy to do. I didn't want to let people within the business down. I felt a bit stuck and decided I would pray to God for guidance and to help get me out of the business. It took three years but eventually the business closed down. I was now able to devote more time and effort to what was consuming me: my faith and my desire to get closer to God, and to know and love Him back, the way He loves us.

It always puzzled me, when I got deep into the Catholic faith, what exactly was I supposed to be doing? There are so many different devotions like the Divine Mercy, the Legion of Mary, Adoration and St Vincent de Paul. There are a lot of groups trying to pull you this way or that way and there are many devotions to various things. I knew I couldn't do them all and so I decided that the first thing I would do, would be to stick to my original instructions on the back of the picture of Our Lady.

I have had so many wonderful experiences in Medjugorje. Any time I go, the sun is always shining and it is always easier to pray when the sun is shining. It is so natural over there because everyone talks about and is interested in the faith. At the Mass, everybody gives answers to the responses, as if it meant something to them. It is a joy to behold. There is so much to do over there that is related to faith but also very enjoyable. It's so natural to be a Catholic in Medjugorje and there is nobody hiding, or just going to Mass on a Sunday and walking out and leaving it behind. It is practised every day over there and you meet so many really beautiful people. The place is an endless joy.

For me, being in a wheelchair, it can be quite challenging sometimes, but I can do almost everything except climb the mountains. However, I was carried up Krizevac in a chair, one time, by the men from the Cenacolo community. God only knows how they did it because the conditions were absolutely treacherous and I really didn't think we would get down safe. But we did. I don't know where the lads got their strength from. It just goes to show that nothing is impossible in Medjugorje, especially if you have God in your life.

I still can't understand why we abandon Him so much; we have a family in heaven, who created heaven and earth, who can do everything and anything; who can take care of every problem you could possibly contemplate and who can look after your every need in ways you couldn't possibly know. How we can't see that as the truth and embrace it and want it in our lives is a bit peculiar to me. As a young man, I always felt that religion was there to restrict your ability to do things. Now, I know that it is only there to restrict you in doing things that are bad for you; things that will make you unhappy. It is there to try and guide you to do things that will make you, and all those around you, happy. It really is a love affair.

For a while after I first came to Medjugorje, my relationship with God and Our Lady was a bright, happy honeymoon period. As I got to know God and Our Lady more, like in all relationships, they became more challenging. However, it deepens your love for each other and deepens your faith and strengthens everything. If you can go through it all and keep going, you become stronger and stronger. When I have a tough day or a hard period, I see God looking me in the eye and saying, 'Right Alan, do you really love me?' If I abandon Him there and then, I am saying, 'I don't love you.' But if I keep praying away and get through the period of telling Him that no matter how things are in life, I still want to love Him; it is an absolutely joyful experience. Although I had a basic faith when I started out, Medjugorje lit a light inside of me that made it all real and brought it to life, making sense of all the bits and pieces I had learned along the way as a child. You can feel God's presence in Medjugorje and the more you feel it, the more you realise that it is true and real and not in people's imaginations. The more you become committed to it and allow it into your life, the more joy and happiness fills up in your heart. While you are learning to love God, He is teaching you to love your neighbour as well, and that boils down to everything we need to do – that is, love God and love your neighbour. We seem so consumed these days with trying to love ourselves, that we have no time for loving anybody else. Other people have to love us for us to feel loved and the more people you love, the more people will love you back, the more you will feel loved yourself.

What does Medjugorje mean to me?

I go back every year to Medjugorje and if I could, I would go back twice a year because every time I go back, I get something more out of it. It recharges my whole being and further strengthens me for the journey of life. It is not an easy journey, and when you are disabled, it can be very challenging. As a result, you need plenty of boosts and the place in this world where you are guaranteed to get a boost to your faith is Medjugorje. If your heart is open to God there, He will fill it with every blessing, every joy and every happiness, and He will teach you how to be a true child of God, if you want it.

10

Mervyn Stokes

AUSTRALIA

Mervyn Stokes has made the long journey from Australia to Medjugorje nine times. In 1991, he had a very visual experience when making his descent down Apparition Hill.

This is Mervyn's testimony.

I have been to Medjugorje nine times, spread over a period of twenty-three years. Our Blessed Mother just keeps calling me back, time after time. I keep telling friends about all the benefits and graces one receives from visiting Medjugorje. Every time I return home, I seem to have the Blessed Mother in my heart. She has not left me for twenty-three years. She encourages me to go to Holy Mass every day, to pray the rosary and to have regular confession. I really love being in Medjugorje, enjoying the graces I receive and praying the rosary with thousands of others – what joy it brings to my heart! When I return home, I can not help but share with others the joy of visiting the village.

The miracle of all this is finding the money to go. I am retired on a pension and a small moderate superannuation fund, which I share with my wife. Every time I decide to go, the money seems to become available for my pilgrimage. Travelling to Medjugorje from Australia, costs, on average, five and a half thousand dollars.

During my visits, I have received many signs and wonders such as the sun spinning, exiting rays and shapes of different colours. I can look at the sun after each evening Mass and it appears to me as a huge, clear-white Eucharist. One night after Holy Mass, I saw the sun turn totally blood red.

Perhaps one of my greatest testimonies occurred during my first visit to Medjugorje which was in August 1991. I was with three other people from West Australia. The civil war was raging. One could hear bombs exploding and the sound of gunfire in the areas surrounding Medjugorje. But we were at total peace and with full faith and trust in Our Lady, we managed to get in and out without any trouble whatsoever. What can I say but that Our Lady was protecting us and looking after us.

On 14 August 1991, the four of us climbed the Hill of Apparitions with the late Fr Slavko. He was a well-loved and truly remarkable priest. We climbed with hundreds of other pilgrims and prayed the rosary. After reaching the top, everyone began to descend. For some unknown reason, the four of us separated from the group and decided to follow another path down the hill on our own.

It was here that a great miracle occurred. The sun began spinning and pulsating over our heads and returning to its original position. It gave off different coloured rays and shapes resembling hearts. The colour of the ground below us turned to gold. This phenomenon lasted for fifteen minutes. After the sun stopped spinning, another great miracle occurred; Our Lady appeared to the four of us for about ten seconds. She was standing in a cloud moving slowly towards and then away from us. The distance from us would be some four to five metres. We could see her very clearly from the knees to the top of her head. She floated in the air towards us with her hands in prayer. As she passed by and started to ascend, it was then that she disappeared.

Looking back at the sun, who did we see in the horizon but Jesus. Because of the vast distance he appeared to be the size of a one-metre statue. He remained in the distance with His hands outstretched as if blessing us for about ten seconds. He then disappeared.

I managed to survive a massive cancer operation after one of my visits to Medjugorje in 1995; I was cleared of cancer after the operation. My physician could not believe it, he was amazed. However, I knew the answer.

11

Sr Colette

IRELAND

Sr Colette is Mother Abbess of the Poor Clare nun's in Galway. As a young woman she graduated as an accountant, had a healthy social life and a few boyfriends. After watching a video on Medjugorje she became intrigued by the story of the apparitions and ended up visiting the village for the first time in 1988. During the consecration at Mass she had a profound encounter with God and this paved the way for her to make the decision to enter the enclosed order some years later. Medjugorje was not only the catalyst that transformed Sr Colette's life, but the faith within her family too.

This is Sr Colette's testimony.

I first heard about Medjugorje at my friend Maura's house. Maura and her father had borrowed a video about the apparitions of Our Lady there. Having grown up with stories of Lourdes and Fatima, I was utterly fascinated by the video. Shortly after that, Fr Slavko came to Ireland and spoke in the Abbey, the Franciscan church in Galway. Again, I was spellbound as the story of Medjugorje unfolded. After that talk, I got a book about Medjugorje and another with the messages in it, and I began trying to live them in my own way.

I should explain that I would not have described myself as very religious. I grew up in a fairly normal Irish Catholic home. I never gave up the practice of the faith, but it didn't go much beyond Sunday Mass and trying to do stuff for Lent. I did become more fervent around exam times, doing novenas to St Anthony and St Joseph of Cupertino – anyone that I felt could swing it for me. At this point in my life, I was studying accountancy, which entailed working full-time in an office, and studying for exams twice a year. I always ended up 'cramming' for exams, so I needed any help I could get.

I heard about a monthly Medjugorje Mass which was held in Galway, and Maura and I began attending it. This whetted my appetite for Medjugorje all the more, as I was exposed to people sharing their experiences of it. Working as a trainee accountant, I didn't earn that much and most of what I did earn went on my social life. I wanted to go to Medjugorje, but not enough to save for it! However, we eventually decided to go at the end of July.

In the meantime, my younger sister Louise got an opportunity to go there in June of that year. She was still in school and was really just treating it as a chance to go on a sun holiday. She was hooked on several TV soaps and had left a list of the ones she wanted recorded while she was away. We forgot to record several of them and knew from past experience that she would not be impressed, to put it mildly. However, when she got back, she told us that she had had a wonderful week there, and she didn't mind at all that we hadn't recorded the programmes. We were flabbergasted, as it was so unlike her. It was quite obvious to us all that she had been touched in a very deep way and I think I found her response to the TV programmes more convincing than anything else I had heard. I felt that something must really be happening in Medjugorje, to have brought about such a profound transformation in her. She worked very hard that summer, as she wanted to save up so that she could go back to Medjugorje in autumn. Meanwhile, I was really looking forward to my trip there the following month.

Eventually, our time to go came. Being the end of July, it was extremely hot. I love sunshine, but it really was hard to take. We launched into the pilgrimage with gusto, climbing a mountain every day and going to everything that was on. We got up very early most days and we would often climb a mountain before breakfast! There were twenty-four pilgrims in our house and there was a great dynamic among us.

Several things stand out for me from that first pilgrimage. One of them was when we went to visit the village where Fr Jozo was ministering. One of the tour guides gave her testimony. She was a convert from Islam and spoke movingly of what her conversion to Christianity had cost her, being virtually cut off from her family. At the end of her story, she thanked us for being her brothers and sisters.

I was deeply touched and really sobbed during her talk, as I realised how much I took my faith and God for granted. Another thing that really stood out for me was my experience of confession. To be honest, I can't remember exactly what I confessed that day. It was more like a feeling of coming home that I had experienced. I know that a lot of people would not have thought that I had ever strayed away from the Church, as I had always continued the practice of the faith. But that day, it felt as if the Father was looking out for me and when He saw me coming, He ran towards me and took me back, just as He had done in the parable of the prodigal son. I felt I made a really good confession and again, I cried very much. It was as if I was cleansed at a very deep level and was accepted again by God. It was such a freeing and liberating experience and I felt so light and joyful within myself.

However, it seemed both of these experiences were a prelude to a profound encounter with God that would change my life. It happened during the consecration at Mass. I had often heard that God loves each one of us, though it meant nothing to me. But in an instant, I was swept off my feet. I felt utterly loved by God and knew for certain that Jesus was truly present in the Blessed Sacrament. I was totally overcome and could not believe the intense feelings of love that I had for God. I cannot even begin to explain the deep feelings of peace and joy that I felt. Nothing in my life compared with it. I had gotten a great love for prayer, because now, it was not just some dry formula that I had to repeat, but a living relationship with someone whom I loved with my whole heart and who I knew loved me.

When I came home from Medjugorje, I spoke to Fr Des O'Malley, a Franciscan priest who was based in Galway, about my experiences. At that stage, I loved God so much, that I wanted to do whatever He wanted, *even* if it meant becoming a nun. I was hoping that I wouldn't have to but I was open to whatever the Lord wanted for me. He suggested that I finish out my studies and look at the vocation later.

Well, I was delighted with that bit of advice, because it meant I could continue to enjoy my life and not have to look seriously at a vocation at that particular moment. In hindsight, it was very wise, because I was not ready to be a nun at that stage. Louise, Maura and I became very involved with a youth prayer meeting in Galway, which was being held in the home of Des and Pat Mannion. It attracted big crowds, with up to one hundred young people there many nights. We made many new friends and it was a great blessing to have young people to share our faith with. We also often socialised together. My mother began attending an adult meeting which was also held in Mannion's on a different night.

As I mentioned earlier, my sister had planned to return to Medjugorje. My mother decided she would like to go as well, so they went together in September of that year with a group from Galway, including her best friend, whom she also persuaded to go. My mother loved it too, so the three of us all became great fans of Medjugorje. My other sister, Nicola, was studying Law in Dublin at that time. She had been working in London during the summer, and so had missed the transformation that had happened to us. She didn't know what hit her when she got home, with all the holy talk! My poor father was living with us, so he had seen it all happening. When we had friends coming around to the house, he used to take up the newspaper and 'tune out' – he didn't have great hearing, which was an advantage. Nicola had about a week at home before she returned to Dublin. I think she was relieved to be going back.

When Nicola came home for Christmas, she had a longer time with us and got a chance to meet and socialise with some of our new friends. Little by little, she was becoming fascinated by it all, though she wouldn't let on that she was. Unbeknown to us, she began exploring her faith a bit more when she returned to Dublin. In the meantime, Our Lady was also working on my dad. He was giving me a lift one day and just said, 'I think I will go to Medjugorje on Thursday.' I couldn't believe it. He had obviously already booked it, but didn't want to let on to us until the last minute. That was the April after we had all gone.

I can remember his return so well. He stayed that night with his sister in Trim. We all spoke to him on the phone and he told each of us, individually, that he loved us. Of course, we knew it already, as both he and my mother had always done everything they possibly could for us, but it was still amazing to hear him saying it. When he got home, he rang Nicola and said that he felt she too should go to Medjugorje and that he would pay for her to go. I think hearing it from dad bore more weight than when we spoke about it. He had been her ally in not being too interested in all the religious 'stuff' and now he too had experienced a great peace in Medjugorje, and it whetted her appetite to go there.

The youth prayer group that we were involved with planned to go to Medjugorje together that summer, for the youth festival, so I felt I would like to go with them. Nicola and Louise also decided to go, and this would be Nicola's first time going. We were very excited to be going together, the three of us and we had great fun packing. We all wore the same size in clothes and often shared them with each other. So we packed all of our summer clothes and as we packed, we'd remind each other of different things we might need to bring. I can remember asking them if they had packed their passports. Nicola is the most organised of all our family and I almost felt stupid reminding her and, needless to say, it was one of the first things she had rooted out when she began to pack. We organised a bus to bring us to Dublin Airport and began to check in when we arrived. It was at this stage that Nicola missed her passport. Unfortunately, when she was packing, she had left something down on top of it and so, it was left at home. We all felt so sorry for her, as it was to have been her first trip. My mother even said she would drive to Dublin with it, if they would hold the plane, but they couldn't. The flight company said that she could go the following week, and only have to pay €50 for it. There was another girl who was also due to go and didn't have a passport either, so they were both left behind and went the following week together. When it was confirmed that they couldn't travel with us, Louise and I raided her luggage, to see what other clothes we could bring with us, assuring her that we would leave them over there for her. It was awful leaving them behind, but she did go the following week, and her life was profoundly touched while there.

This was quite a different trip to the first one. About fifty of us went in all, spread over two weeks and it was wonderful to go there as a group. However, it involved a lot more responsibility for me than when I had gone with my friend. We had many experiences there: most pleasant but some very challenging. It was wonderful to see how Our Lady was working to touch the hearts of all these young people and lead them to her Son.

Having now been well and truly bitten by the Medjugorje 'bug', I saved to return there one more time. As it turned out, this was to be my last time, though I didn't realise it at the time. I returned the following year for Easter Week and it was very special to be there for Divine Mercy Sunday, which was a day of special grace for me. I again travelled with my friend Maura, along with another friend, Martina; my father and aunt were also on the same trip. One thing that stands out for me about that trip was going to Fr Svet for confession, which was so helpful. One of the things he said to me on that occasion was to consider religious life, as it was such a fulfilling way to live. I took what he said on board, but didn't feel it was for me at that stage.

I eventually qualified as an accountant and it seemed then as if the Lord started giving me little hints about religious life. I knew I had to start looking at it more seriously. Shortly after qualifying, I went on holiday to Italy. While in Assisi, I felt that I was being called to the Poor Clare way of life. I got an opportunity to meet with one of the sisters in the monastery there and this was very helpful. When I returned home, I began to look more seriously at the vocation issue. At this point in time, I had a few friends who were also discerning vocations to the priesthood and religious life. I knew that I would eventually have to talk to my family about it, but I dreaded broaching the subject, as I knew they would find it very hard, especially given that I was considering an enclosed order. However, it was only fair to tell them, so one evening I met my sister for a bite to eat after work and told her. I felt that she would be able to help me tell the others, as I had always relied on her strength. However, she broke down and began to cry in the restaurant. I knew that it was going to be awful telling the rest of them, given her response. We went home and told the rest of the family. It was dreadful, as I had expected.

The day after I told them, my father was giving me a lift to work. He told me, with tears in his eyes, that whatever I did, he was proud of me. I was so glad of the moral support of having him behind me, but it broke my heart to see him cry and to know that I was causing my whole family such pain. I felt that it was my fault that they were suffering so much and yet, I knew deep down it was something I had to do.

The following weekend, I went away – I needed a break. My sister gave me a letter as I was leaving. I remember taking it out to read it in a coffee shop and the tears spilling down my face as I read the very moving words about her inner struggle with my decision. It was heartbreaking for me. At that stage, it would have been so much easier to put the whole idea on indefinite hold, but there was no turning back the clock. When I went to Mass that Sunday, I got great consolation from a reflection that was printed in the parish newsletter. I was convinced, when I read it, that the Lord was with me and knew what I was going through. The reflection went as follows:

> Life's most painful choices are not always between good and evil. If that were so, there would be a lot fewer quitters. No, the most painful choices are often between the good and the best. In other words, the things that tempt us to abandon our goals are not always bad. More often than not they are good, and that is what makes it so hard to resist them. We forget what was once precious to us and exchange it for something else that is less good but more immediate. If we wish then to remain faithful, we must be prepared to meet difficulties, especially from inside ourselves. We have to go forward at such times in bare faith, simple hope, and love without sentiment.

The next few months were difficult. Eventually, I applied to the Poor Clares and was accepted. It was a decision that I had to make in faith. God had given little hints, but no big signs. I can see now that He was asking me to take a leap of faith and to trust that He would give me reassurance afterwards. That is one of His many ways of making our faith grow.

A few months after I joined the community, my mother got cancer and had to have major surgery. It was a time when my beliefs were really put to the test. I believed that prayer was all-powerful and now I was given an opportunity to put that belief into practice. And the Lord blessed that in a marvellous way. On a rational level, it might have made more sense to go home and look after my mother, but I entrusted her to God. And He looked after her. She said afterwards that she really felt carried by prayer. It was a great turning point for my entire family, as even up to the time I entered the community, they found it difficult to deal with. Now, at least, they found it easier to accept. Since then, they see that I am happy and they are happy for me. Over the years, they have come to a deep appreciation of our way of life and are very supportive, which has been a great blessing for me.

.   It has not always been easy, but then I never expected that it would be. I didn't think I was coming to a holiday camp. I knew I was committing myself to a radical way of living the Gospel and I wanted to live as fully for God as was possible. It is a wonderful vocation, living as we do, with our lives centred on Christ in the Eucharist. We carry all people in our hearts, and present them daily to the Lord. I have never regretted coming here. I thought, before I joined, that I was making a big sacrifice and doing a great thing in giving myself to the Lord. However, the more I live this life, the more I see that it is I who am on the receiving end, with God endlessly showering His love upon me. Everything has been a huge gift of grace, and I want to spend my life in thanksgiving to God for that.

So, what can I say that Medjugorje means to me? If I were to try and put it in a nutshell, I think I would have to say it is the home of my vocation. It is where I encountered the Lord in a real, life-changing way and I have never looked back since. I also encountered the gentle way that Our Lady works in our lives, leading us to her Son, while staying in the background. I am forever grateful to both of them for what I received there.

12

Chuck Crowe

USA

Chuck Crowe hails from Denver, Colorado. He first visited Medjugorje back in 1990 and credits that first visit with his journey of spiritual conversion. When he travelled to the village for a second time, six years later, he was facing a much harder time in his life. Not only had he been through a divorce and painful back surgery, but he was also battling cancer. During this second trip, Chuck had a profound experience during and after Mass one day, and he felt a healing take place. At the time of writing this testimony, he remains cancer-free.

This is Chuck's testimony.

My name is Chuck and I come from Denver, Colorado. Denver is a long way away from what was then known as Yugoslavia. In fact, it was over twenty-six hours travelling by bus and plane, not to mention the ten hour time difference from the Rocky Mountains.

I thought that my first visit to Medjugorje, in the spring of 1990, would be a simple trip, much like any other. However, I soon discovered it was the beginning of my spiritual conversion, which ultimately changed my life.

Initially, I had gone to Medjugorje hoping that my girlfriend at the time would convert to Catholicism so that we could get married. However, that wasn't in God's plan and shortly after our return, we split up.

I was raised in a large Catholic family, with eleven children and when I heard about the events which were happening in Medjugorje, I believed that they were both profound and serious. I wondered what the meaning of these events was, and what the messages meant for the world and for me.

When I came back from Medjugorje after my first visit, I began to seek a way to live the messages and I found great support in my church. I went to weekly prayer meetings and became more active in my church. I worked tirelessly as a volunteer during Pope John Paul II's visit to Denver for World Youth Day in 1993, when over three hundred thousand visitors descended upon the city of Denver from all around the world.

As time went by, my thinking began to change and what used to hold my attention, like fast cars and business success, no longer seemed that important to me. I married and soon my wife and I had identical twin girls. I named one of them Mirjana, after the visionary in Medjugorje.

All during this time, even though few people knew about the village, I always kept Medjugorje in the front of my mind, whilst trying my best to live the messages.

In March 1996, on my second pilgrimage to Medjugorje, I was facing a much harder time in my life. My marriage had broken down. I was now divorced and my daughters were living in another state. Nine days before the trip, I had undergone surgery to fix my back after it had been damaged in a serious car accident in 1991. On top of all that, one year earlier, in 1995, I had begun treatment after being diagnosed with stage 2 bladder cancer.

I was thinking that I wasn't going to live much longer and I wanted to go back to Medjugorje one last time, to give thanksgiving for my spiritual conversion which had taken place six years earlier. I wanted to pray for the grace and strength needed to face the difficult days ahead.

When I arrived in Medjugorje, the strong, bitter March winds greeted me with a cold, hard rain. It was the kind of weather that no one would want to go out in, not even the hearty Bronco fans. I was suffering excruciating pain and would never have coped if it wasn't for the support of the prayer group I was travelling with. For the first two days, I felt sick and exhausted and all I could do was stay in my room and sleep. On the third day, I realised I was missing everything and so I forced myself out of bed and headed down to the church of St James.

I remember going to Mass in St James' and I immediately felt the Holy Spirit upon me. Tears started pouring down my face. I felt embarrassed and tried to stop crying, but I couldn't. People from my group saw me and began to console me but I wasn't sad or remorseful. The tears came because I had never felt such love before in my life – it was the incredible feeling of God's love. These tears washed away my false pride because I had never wanted anyone to see me cry but I just couldn't help it. It was inside the church, during the Mass, that I believe I was healed.

After Mass, I headed to Cross Mountain, which was an amazing journey climbing all those rocks. I couldn't believe I was able to make it all the way to the top. Once up there, I just stood still and stared at the Cross. A man who looked like he was in his early forties approached me. He was a nice man, dressed in regular clothes, and he said to me, 'It seems you are pretty happy you made this trek up here.' I replied, 'Oh yeah, you wouldn't believe what I have been through, I just had back surgery nine days ago.' The man proceeded to tell me how inspiring it was for him to see me make it and he asked if he could take a picture. He told me he was a Catholic priest. I said he could, and gave him my camera. I never asked him his name and never saw him again.

I felt so happy standing up on the mountain and whilst there, I prayed and thanked the Lord for the strength to physically make it to the top because I knew that this in itself was a small miracle.

Soon after the climb, the pain in my back seemed to diminish and I felt something had changed in me. I felt like I was on the road to recovery. When we came down from the mountain, the group and I went to Vicka's house to hear her speak. Somehow, I managed to get up to the front of the crowds and Vicka came over to me, put her hands on my head and began to pray. Immediately, I felt a surge of energy that was unlike any sensation I ever felt before. It was like electricity flowing from the top of my head down to my toes and it was an overwhelmingly good feeling.

A few days later, the group and I took a bus trip to St Elisha's Church where we met Fr Jozo. He, too, prayed over me and I felt the same type of feeling, like a sensation of electricity, flowing through my body. I knew then that by the grace of God I had been healed but I did not hear or see anything, I just had an inner feeling of peace and wellness.

On the trip home, I felt much better. It wasn't an instant healing, like many people think it would be, but gradual. Eventually, all my pain went away. Although I had started off with a limp in my leg, I continued to walk and exercise and it went away. I had no pain at all and to this day I remain cancer-free.

In total, I have travelled to Medjugorje five times. I feel close to the Blessed Mother over there and being close to her brings me closer to Jesus.

Through my long conversion process, I noticed people kept coming into my life, and later, I could see that God was using me as an instrument. I knew God had a mission for me.

In 1999, I began working in prison ministry to bring the Gospel of Jesus to prisoners. While witnessing in a prison ministry and going inside the Denver prisons isn't easy, I see the rewards of teaching the inmates about Jesus, and about the meaning of faith and hope. After all, that is the least I can do, because I am absolutely sure that if it wasn't for the Blessed Mother and her son Jesus, I wouldn't be here today.

13

Rocco Musumeci

USA

Rocco Musumeci worked for many years as a New York City fireman. His son Georgie became very ill shortly after birth and would have up to two hundred seizures a day. His daughter Alexa was diagnosed with Leukemia before she reached her second birthday. Things were very tough for the family and one night Rocco caught the end of a programme called, Unsolved Mysteries *which talked about a place called Medjugorje where the Virgin Mary was appearing and people were being healed. Rocco made the decision to bring Georgie to Medjugorje and while he was there had numerous meaningful experiences.*

This is Rocco's testimony.

My name is Rocco Musumeci and I am from Great Neck, New York. I was married on 8 September 1985, and my wife and I had three children. Rocky was born in 1987, Georgie was born in 1991, and Alexa was born in 1993. Georgie was born healthy and was circumcised on the second day after his birth. He got a staph infection on the third day after his circumcision. He had to stay in the hospital for about three weeks and had many complications. He became developmentally delayed, had mild Cerebral Palsy and had seizures, as many as two hundred a day. When Rocky was six years old, Alexa was born. She was very healthy and Rocky and Alexa played with Georgie all the time and loved him very much.

I was a New York City fireman, and had been injured when a roof collapsed while I was in a fire. I had neck surgery in June 1994 and was in the hospital for about seven days. When I came out, my wife Kathy noticed Alexa's skin pigment was very pale and that her energy level over the previous days wasn't the same as usual. We took her to the pediatrician's office for some blood work to be done, and were then sent to the hospital for further tests. Alexa was nineteen and a half months old when they diagnosed her with leukemia. Everything seemed like it was falling apart. I always read my bible and I prayed for help from God because my hands were tied. However, before all of this came into play, I had stopped going to church due to an issue I had with a priest before my wedding and I blamed the whole church for it.

Four months later, I came out of my neck brace. In the meantime, Alexa was on chemotherapy and several other treatments, including blood transfusions. We almost lost her a few times, especially after a twenty-three-day stay in the hospital. In 1995 she spent fifty days in the hospital and Georgie spent twenty-five days there.

In November of 1995 at 1:30 a.m., I could not sleep, so I went downstairs and put on the television. There was a show on called *Unsolved Mysteries* and it was about a place called Medjugorje, where the Virgin Mary was appearing and people were being healed one way or another. I caught the end of the show, but it never said where Medjugorje was. I asked around to see if anyone knew of Medjugorje, but no one did. So it started to slowly slip from my mind.

One day in January of 1996, my wife yelled out, 'I found it!'

'Found what?' I replied.

'That place Medjugorje you were talking about, it's in Bosnia.'

'Bosnia,' I said, 'there's no way I'm going there!'

Two months later, I got my first book on Medjugorje. It was the first book I had ever read in its entirety. Then, I caught myself reading three books about Medjugorje in the space of a month; a complete miracle.

I had decided to go to Medjugorje and take Georgie there with me and leave Rocky and Alexa home with their mother because Alexa was on treatments. Before we were to leave, I took Georgie to the doctor to see if there was any possible way for him to get brain surgery in order to stop his seizures. The day that I took him to be checked out was the feast day of St George, 23 April 1996. The doctor told me there was nothing he could do, as Georgie had a lot of damage done to his brain already and stopping the seizures seemed impossible.

I didn't want to go on a pilgrimage but from that moment on, I knew it was time for me to just go for it and book my trip; since I had nothing to lose. I looked into how to get there. I got a phone call from a tour operator on 26 May 1996 and they said there was an opening for two people in June, and so I took it. In the meantime, Georgie was on a ketogenic diet, which was a diet filled entirely with fatty foods that would lessen the amount of seizures from two hundred to twenty-five a day. Knowing there was a war in Bosnia and Herzegovina, I decided to bring along extra clothing with me to give away to those who needed it. The tour operator gave me a list of things to bring, such as a backpack, rain gear, a water bottle and climbing boots.

When we finally arrived at JFK airport in New York, we were to meet sixteen other people coming from different states. The group leader was a girl called Jackie, from Louisiana. When I met Jackie at the airport and introduced myself to her, she said to me, 'How did you get these tickets? I have many people in line for them.' I said, 'I really don't know.'

We became really good friends and she helped me with Georgie, watching out for him as if she was his own grandmother; that's why I called her Grandma Jackie. Jackie introduced Georgie and me to the rest of the group and everyone was so nice, but seemed a little scared, or didn't know what to expect with Georgie being so handicapped. Georgie was in diapers, he couldn't walk or talk, and the seizures were very obvious. You could see the fear in their eyes for him. However, Georgie's eyes were pure love and, within days, everyone melted and loved him, especially Helen from Illinois.

As with us, it was Helen's first trip to Medjugorje and she didn't know what to expect. She told me she had a dream a few days before she went to Medjugorje, that a little boy would change her life. At the end of the ten-day trip, she told me that that little boy was Georgie. While we had a layover stop to Medjugorje in Rome, Jackie spotted the bishop of New Orleans. I decided to take Georgie to him and get him blessed. I was going to ask every priest I saw to bless him. I was determined to make this trip worthwhile in any way I could to benefit Georgie.

I made a deal with the Blessed Mother that I would do anything she told me to, if she fixed Georgie up. It was a long time since I went to confession, so I decided to do it in Medjugorje. I went to Mass, read my bible, and fasted on bread and water on Fridays, although I didn't do the rosary, as I thought it was for old ladies. I used to sit with my grandmother on her couch and watch TV while she prayed the rosary; which is why I thought it was a grandma kind of thing. Well, now you can call me grandma, because I pray the rosary every day. I didn't know how to pray the rosary; when we flew from Rome to Split in Croatia, there was a four-hour bus ride to Medjugorje and everyone prayed the rosary while Georgie and I sat there listening. I knew I was in the right place with the right people, but I still felt very embarrassed.

We arrived in Medjugorje on 1 June 1996 at 10 p.m. When everyone got off the bus, I noticed they had been looking up at the sky. I looked up and saw a large bright halo around the moon. I had never seen a full moon that looked like that. Reading the books on Medjugorje, there were many things that people saw there. 'If I could look at the sun without hurting my eyes,' I told myself, 'I will believe the Blessed Mother is appearing here.' I didn't know then that I was a doubting Thomas.

We stayed in a house where a man named Ivan and his wife Veronica took good care of us all. They both helped me with Georgie all week as I came in and out of the house with his strollers. Everyone prepared to go to church the next day, as it was Saturday. I put our suitcases in our bedroom and unpacked and left the two give-away suitcases in the corner and asked God to tell me who to give them to. I looked out the window, into the fields outside the house and said, 'What am I doing here? I must be going crazy.'

I had a good night's sleep, got up at eight in the morning and went downstairs for breakfast. Ivan and Veronica put out a delicious meal and everyone ate and was very excited to be there. We had a priest on the pilgrimage named Fr Dominic, and I made sure he blessed Georgie as many times as possible. I was planning on going to confession, but not to him because I had so many sins that I would have felt ashamed to see him every day afterwards. So my plan was to find a priest whom I would never see again. We all walked to the church and arrived at 10 a.m. The church was packed and we all split up. Georgie and I stayed in the back corner of the church.

I didn't receive Communion because I had not gone to confession yet. After Mass, when almost everyone had left, Georgie and I moved more up closer to the front pews. I started to cry uncontrollably for no reason. Maybe it was the grief that I had for not going to Mass all these years and blaming the Church. Maybe it was because I was in a church, asking for a favour for my son that I didn't deserve to get. Helen saw me there and came over and asked if I was ok. I was crying so hard that I couldn't even talk. I just waved to her as if to ask her to leave, so she left and now I began to feel even worse.

About a half an hour went by and I decided to leave the church. I felt like I was in the desert, looking around. I didn't know where to go. There was a Franciscan store next to the church and I decided to go in and buy souvenirs for people back home. I was looking around, buying rosary beads, scapulars and medals and as I was about to leave the store, there was a priest sitting there. I asked him, 'Father, do you know where I can get these blessed?' He said, 'Yes, take them to the church and ask a priest to bless them.' As I was walking out of the store I felt confused and went back in and said to the priest, 'Father can you bless them?' He said, 'I thought you'd never ask!'

His name was Fr Fernando. I got the gifts blessed and then I asked him if he could bless Georgie, which he gladly did. As I left the store, we sat around a flower garden and I fed Georgie his lunch. It took about an hour to feed Georgie a meal; he couldn't chew and everything had to be pure. Fr Fernando passed by us and waved. I said to him, 'Father, will you hear my confession?' He said, 'Yes, let's go.' So I packed everything up and strolled Georgie towards the church. It was about one hundred degrees outside.

There was a bench under a tree. We sat there and I received confession for the first time in twenty-four years. I thought I was going to get scolded after that, but he simply told me to say one Hail Mary for penance, and to say it slow. I felt like I had gotten away with murder. After confession, he told me that there would be a blessing for children the next day after morning Mass and that I should bring Georgie. I said I would try, but I was thinking, 'I just went to Mass today and you want me to go again tomorrow, too?' I felt great after confession, as though I was free of all of the sins I had been carrying for years.

Georgie and I spent the day together, walking around the town and in awe of just being there, in Medjugorje. That night, I went to bed around midnight and a rooster woke me up at 3 a.m. He crowed about fifteen times and my eyes finally opened to the window where there was a star in the shape of a cross. I rubbed my eyes and sure enough, it was a cross. I got out of bed, as Georgie was having a seizure from the loud noise of the rooster. When I got him rested again, I went to the window and the cross was gone. I looked all over and there were only stars. To my surprise, about two hundred yards away, there was a glowing at the second floor window of a house. It was the shape of a man, glowing in the dark while running in place. He took up the whole window but he was not inside the room.

He turned to me and I got a little scared; then he turned back to the front of the house and started running again, while holding something like a big book in his hand. So my head turned towards the front of the house and there was a forty-foot tree, with a woman standing over it. She was about fifty feet tall and was cradling a child in her left arm. I gazed on for about ten minutes or so, before deciding to get a closer look. I went outside to the back of the house and looked at the tree where the woman was. She was not there, nor was the man at the window. I went all over the yard to get a better look, but still, no one was there. I went back to my room and looked out the window and there she was again, along with the glowing man. I stayed up for about forty-five minutes and nothing happened, so I thought that this kind of stuff must happen all the time in this town.

The next morning at breakfast I told everyone about what happened. I didn't know what they were thinking about me but I knew this was real. I was definitely going to church after this. I arrived at the church and it was packed, so Georgie and I sat in the back again. There were nineteen priests on the altar, and to my surprise the main priest was Fr Fernando. As they were giving Communion, all of the priests were in different parts of the church. Fr Fernando was in the front so I decided to try and receive from him, because I had been to confession to him the previous day.

I carried Georgie through the crowd, which seemed to open up as I was moving closer to the front. It was truly amazing how that happened. When Fr Fernando gave the final blessing, he said for all to bring their children to the front for a special blessing. As I carried Georgie to the front and he blessed everyone with holy water, he waved to me to come closer. I went to him and he took Georgie out of my arms, and held him over the altar and said, 'This is Georgie, I consecrate him to God.'

A chorus from Colorado was singing 'Gentle Woman' at the time that this was happening. Fr Fernando held Georgie up for a while, before giving him back to me. As I walked to the back of the church to the stroller, I was crying like a baby.

As the day went on, people came up to me to meet Georgie. Helen said that she knew he was a special boy. A writer from the *Medjugorje Herald*, Ray, asked if his photographer could take a picture of Georgie and me for a story. He put it in the July 1996 issue, and also the October and November issues that same year. Ray also told me that he was going to the city of Mostar to bring food and clothing to the hospital there, which had been badly affected by the war. I immediately knew where my two extra bags of clothing should go.

I went to bed that night feeling so good about Georgie and having high hopes that there would be a good chance for his healing. Again, I was woken by a rooster around 3 a.m. in the morning and ran to the window. There was the glowing man running in the same place and the woman holding the baby in the tree. I stayed at the window, waiting for something to happen for about an hour but nothing occurred. I did not understand this.

At breakfast, I told everyone again what had happened. Half of them were excited, and I think the other half thought I was crazy. I was back in church for the third time in a row – a new record. As a group, we all went to Apparition Hill, where everyone witnessed the miracle of the sun. I could see it with just one eye opened and the other eye closed. When I went to bed that night, I woke up at 3 a.m. on my own with no rooster waking me up this time, and there was no glowing man or woman with the baby.

The rest of the week was full of a grace from heaven that I didn't understand. On one occasion, Helen and I saw the cross spinning on top of Mt Krizevac, as well as a cloud formation of a heart with a red glow in the background. Another day, we climbed Mt Krizevac in ninety-five degrees of heat; all eighteen of us in the group with Grandma Jackie leading the way alongside Fr Dominic. I carried Georgie all the way up and stopped to pray at every station of the cross. At the tenth station I saw the miracle of the sun and it seemed like all of the bushes and greenery turned gold.

Our tour guide followed me up because I was in the back of the group and I believed he was worried for me because I had neck surgery one and a half years earlier and I was now carrying Georgie. When we reached the top I was beat and I sat down with Georgie. Carl from my group came up to me and said, 'There is an Italian group holding hands and praying around the cross at the top of the mountain. You must put Georgie in the middle of that prayer group.' I told him I could not get up, and if he would take Georgie instead, I would be very grateful to him. He did so, and it was so beautiful. We stayed at the top of the mountain for about two hours and then descended. Going down was even harder than going up, because of the rocks and worrying about slipping while carrying Georgie.

The day eventually arrived when we had to leave Medjugorje. We all boarded the bus and everyone was sad to leave. However, I felt ready to go home. We boarded the plane to Rome and the grace from God came back to me and I started to miss Medjugorje. I couldn't wait to go home and tell everyone what had happened to me there. On the journey home, Helen said to me she was convinced Georgie was the little boy who would change her life. She said Georgie had been blessed by everyone and that the only one he hadn't seen was the Pope!

We had a stay over in Rome and spent the night at the Michelangelo Hotel. We were all to meet in the lobby to go to a restaurant for dinner. Georgie and I were running very late due to his seizures so I told the others that I would meet them in the restaurant. About twenty minutes later, I went down to the lobby and everyone had gone except Helen. As we walked down the street, a cavalcade of cars with flashing lights passed us by and then the Popemobile passed. Helen was in amazement, and she kissed Georgie.

The next day, we boarded the plane back to New York and said our goodbyes to everyone in the group, as they were taking other flights back to where they lived. Through the years, I have kept in touch with most of them, especially Grandma Jackie and Helen. Weeks went by, and I prayed, fasted, went to confession often, attended Mass as much as possible, and read the Bible daily along with other Catholic devotions.

Georgie started to get worse with grand mal seizures and started to weaken daily. Three months after I got back from Medjugorje, on 21 September 1996, Georgie passed away in his sleep. He had never had a life-threatening problem, and there was no explanation for his passing. But I instantly knew that the vision I had had in Medjugorje was our Blessed Mother holding Georgie and telling me not to worry, for he would be with her, and would be cured. He had the ultimate healing to be in heaven with the Blessed Mother and her son Jesus, of which I could not contest, and only be thankful for and hope to be with him in paradise one day.

The loss of Georgie was so painful, but I always look forward to the reunion with him. I pray to him always, for he is my link to heaven. The night Georgie died, his mother wrote a beautiful eulogy to him, which was published in the November 1996 issue of the *Medjugorje Herald*. Georgie is buried at the highest point of the cemetery in Roslyn, New York, which is the highest point of the town. Ten feet from him is an identical eight-foot tall cross, like the one on top of Mt Krizevac. I put a bench there and inscribed it as 'Little Mt Krizevac'.

Nine months went by, and Alexa had her last cycle of chemotherapy. Five years have passed and she is now considered cured from leukemia. Rocky has graduated college from the US Merchant Marine Academy and is now a lieutenant in the navy. As these years have passed, I've had nine surgeries on my neck, back, colon, hip, knee and shoulder. I have two more children: Sophia, who is eleven years old, and Andrew, who is nine years old. Sophia has autism and Andrew has Down's syndrome, autism, thyroid problems and type 1 juvenile diabetes. I also took into my home my mother, who has Alzheimer's disease, and my disabled father, to care for.

Whenever things get tough, I hold my son Andrew who, despite all his problems, comforts me with his loving smile. I have gone through these trials and tribulations with a thorn in my side. I hope and pray God will remove it soon but I would like to thank our Blessed Mother for bringing me closer to her son Jesus.

14

Michael Ripple

USA

Michael Ripple is the author of A Lost Shepherd, An Ex-Priest's Journey from Sin to Salvation. *Together with his wife, he leads pilgrimages to Medjugorje and gives talks and retreats on a variety of spiritual topics.*
This is Michael's testimony.

I didn't know I was looking for answers.
I didn't know I had questions.
I thought I had it all …

I was halfway across the world, standing in St James' Church, a structure much too small for the mass of humanity gathered there. People were pressing in on me from all sides. I tried to kneel in adoration of the Holy Eucharist but I couldn't move. I stretched to catch a glimpse of the Blessed Sacrament. A cloud of smoke floated above the altar, creating a display of shadows and light as the incense burned and its scent filled the air. If only the incense could mask the smell of body odour.

I felt another push. An old woman with a brown babushka and arthritic knuckles leaned against me. She thumbed her worn rosary beads and moved her lips in silent prayer.

I glanced over my left shoulder and saw more people pushing in through the huge front doors. I watched from my position in the side aisle. Each person who entered set off a chain reaction that looked like grains of sand slowly shifting positions. More people pushed in, and I was jostled several steps – against my will – until I could no longer hold my place. In a few brief moments, I was involuntarily shoved out the side door by the will of the crowd.

113

I put my hands in the pockets of my worn khaki blazer and felt for my rosary beads as I meandered along the walkway, now worn smooth by the feet of millions of religious pilgrims. 'Just as well,' I thought.

I took a long, deep, deliberate breath, closed my mouth and slowly blew the air out my nostrils. 'I wouldn't have been able to pray in that crowd anyway,' I muttered, in a voice no one else could hear.

Outside, the cool spring air awoke me from my incense-induced stupor. I walked by the entrance and looked up at the clock on the bell tower. It was 10 p.m. on a weeknight and the church was packed for this Eucharistic Adoration. I stood in front of the huge carved wooden doors, which were propped open, and once more caught a glimpse of the altar and the gold monstrance where the round piece of unleavened bread, the presence of the Body of Christ, was safely displayed. The host now appeared to be glowing red as if it was on fire.

I glanced at all the people, hundreds of them, gazing and praying, and I grew envious of their passion. Unlike them, I felt no strong emotion, positive or negative. Yet, we were all sharing a pilgrimage that night. From distant places around the globe, as so many before us, we had travelled here to pray in this small town of Medjugorje, where the Blessed Virgin Mary first appeared to six children on 24 June 1981. Mary was still regularly appearing to three of the original six visionaries. This was the longest-lasting Marian apparition event in the history of the Catholic Church, and her message was simple: Get back to God.

In spite of the area's communist persecution, war, and even some doubtful Croatian bishops, the Mother of God continued to lead her children back to the heart of her son, Jesus. From all religions, millions of people, millions of seekers, millions of sinners were offering prayers in this place. I was now one of millions, but there wasn't room for me tonight.

'I don't even know how to pray anymore,' I mumbled, again to myself.

I made my way to a wooden bench, took a seat and leaned back. Behind me were more benches and a row of outdoor confessionals that reminded me of a small ten-room motel; little cards by the doors indicated the language each priest could accommodate. I now understood why some called Medjugorje the 'Confessional for the World.' For the moment though, no one was in line and there were no priests. It was just me, sitting between the church and the confessionals. I thumbed the rosary and crucifix in my jacket pocket.

'Jesu Christo,' spoke a deep, slow, guttural voice over the loud speaker.

'Jesu Christo,' I repeated to myself. I stood and walked by a statue that resembled a dwarf Franciscan friar.

'Jesu Christo,' the voice said again.

A sacred silence seemed to surround me and I felt the urge to kneel down – alone in the open, dark space.

The sound of an engine broke the silence. Headlights appeared. An old rusty Fiat ran up over the curb and onto the paved stone walkway. The car passed within a few feet of me, screeching to a halt. The passenger doors quickly opened and two Franciscan friars jumped out, left the doors ajar and ran up the steps leading to the back sacristy door, their white rope cinctures dangling behind them. They knocked hard at the door somewhat frantically, with the loud thumps sending echoes into the darkness.

The driver stayed in the car and revved the engine, which continued to putter out a smoky, noxious exhaust. The back sacristy door opened and a crack of light escaped into the night. I watched the silhouette of the friar inside bless himself as the other two shared some seemingly urgent news. With the message apparently delivered, the two friars ran back down the steps and returned to the car. The driver did a tight U-turn and the car sped off as quickly as it had come, again passing just a few feet in front of me.

I shifted my weight from one knee to the other and looked back over my shoulder. I felt as though the dwarf-like friar statue was staring at me. Over the loudspeaker, a voice spoke another prayer, first in Croatian, then in English, 'In thanksgiving for the life and death of our Holy Father.'

Now the driver's urgency and the friar's panic all made sense.

'He died,' I whispered to myself, 'Pope John Paul has died.'

I closed my eyes and remembered him. I had received the sacrament of confirmation the same day he was elected pope. We had his papal blessing for the Ripple family framed and hanging in our home, and I had a prayer card with the picture of his face, a young John Paul. I had shared the priesthood of Christ with Pope John Paul. I was ordained a Roman Catholic priest under his papacy. The same hands that broke the bread and poured the wine, the same hands that healed and blessed the sick, the same hands laid upon the disciples, ordaining them to go forth and proclaim the kingdom of God, those same hands – Jesus' hands – that were placed upon John Paul II, were placed upon me. Tonight, a brother priest died.

Outside the church, in the dark, alone, I knelt on both knees. I had left the very church that ordained me, after having my eyes opened to the darker realities of the priesthood and of myself, after realising I would never fit the model of 'the parish priest'. After being angry at an institution that no longer had room for me or my new life, after being excommunicated – I knelt there, outside the Body of Christ, and I felt empty.

I felt like a lost shepherd.

From a place deep, deep within my soul, a prayer began to form. Effortlessly it passed through my lips as a whisper into the darkness, 'John Paul – pray for me, pray for this priest – ordained under you, now lost, sinful, and forgotten.'

'Pray for me. Pray for my wife. Pray for my son.'

From *A Lost Shepherd*, New Hope Press 2012, Michael Ripple.

What does Medjugorje mean to me?

That was my soul's introduction to Medjugorje. I was on my knees and in the dark.

It wasn't supposed to happen that way. Everything in life was fine. Years earlier, I fell in love and left the Roman Catholic priesthood, the church, and the faith. I was now married to my lovely wife, Wendy, and I was a father to our young son, Isaac. And I could celebrate the sacraments in the Anglican tradition. Life was good. I had a lovely little rectorship in a wealthy parish and the congregation was growing.

That pilgrimage to Medjugorje was supposed to be a nice trip, filled with thanksgiving for Wendy's healing from cancer. That was, after all, the only reason why I went.

Or so I thought …

For five days, I felt disconnected from my family. I knew Wendy was experiencing her own spiritual turmoil but I was completely helpless. For five days, I witnessed miracle upon miracle and sign upon sign. For five days, I wrestled angels and demons. For five days, I lost my voice. Stricken, mute; I had no choice but to listen.

In that desolate, mountainous village, God had provided everything. All I needed to do was surrender my will.

The day before our return home, I spoke with the priest from our group. Even though I was 'excommunicated' (because I had publicly pronounced my conversion to the Episcopal Church in the United States) my old seminary classmate listened to my confession, a confession that took years in the making – I left the Church and I wanted to make things right, not only for my soul, but, more importantly for the souls of my wife and son.

Unbeknownst to me, my loving wife had made the same confession just hours before.

Our Lady of Medjugorje was at work!

It was unusual, at best – a Roman Catholic priest, who became an Episcopalian, now was seeking to return with his wife who was previously married. Mary took our hand, the Holy Spirit orchestrated our return, and a Roman Catholic bishop personally conducted the process.

I still marvel at the simplicity of the miracle of Medjugorje.

It's really about losing one's will. It's about modelling Mary's fiat; 'Be it done unto me.' Surrender and confess the sin of pride and the gates of heaven will open.

When I made that first pilgrimage, I had amassed years of personal justification for the sins I committed as a priest, a husband, and a father. By the time I climbed the hills in Medjugorje I was already spiritually exhausted from years of prideful living.

Eventually I wrote to Pope Benedict XVI:

I seek this dispensation and favour for the salvation of my soul … I did not bring honour or respect to the ministry of priesthood … It has been through this grace-filled process of seeking dispensation that I continue to realise the gravity of my sinful ways … I seek this dispensation and to return because I have a responsibility to provide for the spiritual welfare of my family. I cannot achieve this continuing to live in the current state. Following a pilgrimage my family made to Medjugorje, in thanksgiving to God for my wife's healing from cancer, my wife and I felt called to become reconciled with the Roman Catholic Church. Most Holy Father, I make this request in my own hand …

To this day Medjugorje invites me to humility and it still hurts. For many, Medjugorje can be the wellspring of humility, and true humility gives strength for one to accept martyrdom. I think of the early days of Medjugorje and how the visionaries' lives were at risk. The potential for martyrdom was not out of the question. They were hunted and apprehended and their families risked real humiliation and hardship. It is easy to forget and lose that sense of potential martyrdom in the midst of today's souvenir shops and eateries and modern-day conveniences.

And yet, on this very day and at this very moment, Our Lady of Medjugorje is inviting someone to get on their knees in the dirt and rocks of a hill and become humble before our God.

15

Angela Hayes

IRELAND

Angela Hayes was only thirty-two when she lost her husband, who died by suicide. With four young boys to bring up, life was, at times, very difficult for them. Nine years later, another tragedy struck the family. Whilst trying to cope with more grief and pain in their lives, Angela and her sons were asked to go on a pilgrimage to Medjugorje. Over there, they found peace and it helped them cope with what had happened in their lives.

This is Angela's testimony.

My name is Angela and I am from Kilkenny City in Ireland. In 2002, at the age of thirty-two, I became a widow. My husband, Tommy, had died by suicide. I was a mother to four young boys. Stephen was thirteen, Thomas was ten, Robert was seven and Alan was four. Tommy and I had met at the age of sixteen and married quite young and life was good.

There is no book, there are no words, there is nothing that can prepare you for the turmoil that suicide brings. Our lives had been turned upside down.

We took each day as it came, not knowing what was the best thing to do. How were we going to survive life emotionally and financially without my husband and father of my young boys?

My family and our friends were there to help us get through this painful time. They supported us as best as they could, especially my mum and dad. They were the ones who were there to help pick up the pieces with me and help me carry my cross. They put their arms around me and let me know that everything would be ok.

No one can be prepared for what suicide brings. The pain is an indescribable one that no one on earth should have to witness. But unfortunately we do.

I did my best in bringing up my sons, acting as both a mum and dad and teaching them invaluable life skills. We were just so busy all the time. Life was hard, especially on the boys not having a male role model in their life; no dad to run to at their moments of achievement. It was very difficult for me to see other families together and it was a constant battle each day as to how we would cope. All the occasions like Christmas and birthdays were not easy but we just had to make the most of life.

We had brilliant times together on our camping days. We loved it and I thank God for those treasured memories.

Unfortunately, as time went by, my eldest son Stephen changed. He was finding life so very hard. He was fifteen and had met new friends that seemed to be having fun; more fun than he was having. They didn't have to go to school and they had no worries or cares in the world. Here was another challenge – how was I going to keep Stephen in school?

Stephen had achieved All-Ireland medals for running and was representing Kilkenny in swimming. He played hurling and soccer and was training to be a lifeguard.

Eventually, at the age of seventeen, he left school, but I didn't mind because he had been offered an apprenticeship in carpentry. After a short while, Stephen had lost interest in all of his sports, and he was always meeting up with his new friends after work.

He became dependent on drugs and alcohol and didn't seem to care about himself or anything else, but deep down I knew he was in so much pain. He was hurting because of the way his life had become and because of losing his dad.

Things got so bad that he just wanted to die and be with his dad. I spent terrible nights driving around, crying. I would look for him on the streets and worry whether he was in the river. I didn't know where he was. We were all so frightened for Stephen, and *of* Stephen, and I didn't know how to cope.

I was told about an addiction centre that could help my son, called the Aislinn Centre. Stephen was admitted there for treatment and whilst there, he accepted that he was an addict. It's so hard to watch your children suffer like this through no fault of their own, but at least he was going to get help and work through it all.

In September 2010, life was good for us all and we thought things couldn't have been better. We had come through the worst and we were making the best of life.

Stephen became a father, naming my beautiful new grandson Thomas, after my husband. Life was great, but on 20 March 2011, nine years and a day since my husband's death, the worst, most horrendous thing that can happen to a mother happened to me. I lost my precious son, Thomas, at the age of eighteen, and again his untimely death was due to suicide.

How? Why? I couldn't take this. The pain was just unbearable.

My heart was ripped to shreds. My beautiful son! He was beautiful inside and out and loved by all. He was training as a chef and was a scout leader and had everything going for him. He was caring, bubbly and outgoing. So many people knew him and had great time for him. He never showed any signs of how low he was feeling and how much he was hurting over the death of his dad.

I questioned how this had happened and asked 'what did I do wrong?' But I got great relief in the letter he left for me with words that assured me it was nothing I had done. He said he had just wanted to be with his dad and that he was going to tell his dad all about the great times we had had together, especially our camping days.

Once again, we were faced with how we were going to survive and live life without a son, a brother, an uncle, a cousin and a friend. Our lives fell apart. After all the years of hard work and things finally being better, I simply couldn't understand why this had happened.

After Thomas' death, my sons Stephen and Robert were approached by the local youth group and asked to go to Medjugorje on a youth pilgrimage. Now, religion and God were very far from their minds. They felt let down by God with what had happened. However, Medjugorje was the beginning of them finding peace and learning to live life without Tommy and Thomas.

The following year, in 2012, Stephen said to me 'Mam, you have to go to Medjugorje.' He told me it was amazing and that I would love it. So, that summer I went along with Stephen and my other son Alan as part of the Medjugorje Youth Group.

Medjugorje is different for everyone and there are many stories about the place, but they all have one thing in common – peace. I never witnessed anything like it before and during my time there a weight was lifted off my shoulders. I witnessed a peace in my heart; a true peace. I knew Our Lady was there for me to help carry my burden and I got reassurance that I am never alone.

Medjugorje has been a miracle for my family. The peace and healing my sons and I got when we went there changed our lives by helping us to cope with everyday struggles as best we can. All you need is an open heart and an open mind, and what you will get from Medjugorje is amazing.

Nowadays, I don't let things – or I try not to let things – worry me. I reflect on the serenity of prayer and hand it over to a higher power because at the end of the day, what's meant to be will be. I've realised that there is no point in me getting stressed and worried about things that are out of my control.

Since my husband's death, each Christmas has been a struggle but this year has been a good one for us. My three sons and I seem to be coping better.

Tempting as it was, I could never give up hope and I knew I had to continue for the family that was left behind. We all needed each other. I am such a proud mother of my four sons and my little daughter Caoimhe.

Even after all the pain and hurt, they have turned out to be fine young men that are loving, caring and respectful. This would not be the case if it weren't for their teachers, the Kilkenny bereavement society, the Aislinn Centre, the Kilkenny Medjugorje group, Joe and Fr Mark Condon, and, above all, my family: my sister Linda, my brothers Kevin and Joey, my niece and nephews and my friends.

To finish, all I can say is: if you have been affected by suicide, keep hope, stick with each other and pray. You cannot do it alone. It's early days for us in coping with another huge loss, but we have been given the strength to continue to live, through our loss and pain.

A trust was established in 2014 to commemorate the life of Thomas by financially assisting groups that work in the area of suicide prevention, youth development and counselling.

Details on the trust can be found at www.thethomashayestrust.ie.

Alan Hayes has also released a CD called *Survivor*, which is available from the trust. The CDs cost €5 and all proceeds go to The Thomas Hayes Trust.

16

Keith Kelly

IRELAND

From a young age, Keith Kelly began to get into a lot of trouble in primary school. In his teenage years, this spiraled out of control because of his use of drink and drugs. Although he was unhappy within himself, Keith continued partying hard, which eventually led to him getting expelled from secondary school and got him into much trouble with the police. At eighteen years of age, two weeks before he was to appear in court on eleven charges and face the high possibility of a prison sentence, Keith found himself visiting Medjugorje. Whilst there, he had an experience which saw him turn his life around dramatically.

This is Keith's testimony.

I don't really know where to start. I suppose as a child, I was very sensitive but also a bit of a worrier and a people pleaser. I was more interested in winning the approval of my classmates in school and my friends elsewhere than I was about pleasing God. I had a constant hunger for attention.

The attention-seeking thing in school started to become a bit of a problem and it wasn't long before I was suspended. I was still in primary school and just about to make the transition into secondary school. Getting suspended fed my ever-increasing ego as I sought to fill that void which, I realise now, only God can fill.

I must mention that I don't come from a strongly religious background. We were a Catholic family but in name alone, and we only went to Mass on very special occasions like Christmas, Easter, etc.

Secondary school was an absolute nightmare for my parents. In fact, you could say that my whole teens were, as I took out all of my anger and frustration at not feeling wanted on myself and others, especially my family. I simply wasn't able to find my place in life.

I started drinking and taking drugs, and it wasn't very long before I was in trouble with the law. My parents made regular visits to the police station. At fifteen years of age, when I was at the height of my partying days, I was expelled from school. I really thought that this was the life. However, I became more and more empty inside. I was a very popular guy who was always at the centre of every party and I had everything that I thought I wanted. Inside, I was just dead.

In my later teens, the consequences of taking too many chemicals into my body, began to take its toll. I started to have attacks in the middle of the night, where I would wake up dripping in sweat. I was pinned to the bed, completely paralysed.

At first I thought I was loopy or going nuts but the attacks became more and more frequent, and more and more intense. Soon, it wasn't just at night that I was feeling like this but, in fact, all of the time, so I told my mum. I went to counsellors, psychiatrists, you name it!

After a particularly bad attack one night when I literally woke up the whole house, my mum began to bless my bed with holy water and say the prayer to St Michael. However, the attacks continued. Everything came to a head one night when I looked into the bathroom mirror and saw the type of person I had become. I started to freak out and for ten minutes I could do absolutely nothing of my own accord. I was in tears at this point but somehow I was given the grace to fall to my knees and I began to pray the Our Father. It was probably the only prayer I knew but I really prayed it and I meant every word. I was calling out to my Heavenly Father as if He was really there and halfway through the prayer, I just felt this force come down upon me and cast out all the darkness I had been feeling. I can remember just lying there crying, enveloped in this divine peace.

That was the moment when I realised that God was there and that He had always been there. I realised that He doesn't abandon us but rather we abandon Him. From that moment on, I began to pray to God on a daily basis, begging Him for help. I had a court case looming and I was up for eleven charges. My solicitor told me that I was looking at a possible prison sentence.

Two weeks before my court appearance, I found myself on a plane going to Medjugorje. Jim, the group leader, had told my father that he would take any member of my family except me. However, he eventually succumbed, due to my father's persistence. My dad was determined to help get me better, although I knew deep down that he thought I was a lost cause. Thankfully, Our Lady didn't.

I must admit, it wasn't all plain sailing, and I spent the first couple of nights in Medjugorje drinking. I wasn't really participating in the organised activities, but on the third day I climbed Apparition Hill with my dad, my sister, my aunt and the rest of our group. We began to pray the rosary. It is very hard to put into words what happened to me when we were halfway up Apparition Hill, but I will try.

I can only describe it as a warm, unconditional embrace from my heavenly mother. It was for me, her straying, prodigal son. It broke down all my defenses, swept me off my feet and melted my heart. From that moment on, I promised her that I would pray the rosary every day as a sign that I belong to her and as a gesture of my love and gratitude. I truly believe that it was this moment which saved me and kept me on the straight and narrow – the fact that I never let go of Our Lady's hand.

My favourite quote is from Bishop Fulton Sheen, which says, 'A soul cannot remain in the state of sin and pray the rosary at the same time. Either he will give up sin or give up praying the rosary.'

The power of prayer was very evident on the day of the court case. I didn't know what to expect and to be honest, I feared the worst. However, once again, I felt that God came to my rescue in extraordinary circumstances. I had only just turned eighteen and this meant that the court case was public and that I would have to take the stand. The police wouldn't let me speak and kept interrupting me. They were fed up with me and just wanted me behind bars. Remarkably, the judge sent the police out of the courtroom so that I was able to speak.

I just poured out my heart and told her everything about my experience in Medjugorje. The judge gave me one more chance. I was given community service and a curfew where I had to check in at a particular time every night for a year. This didn't bother me, as this was the miracle I was asking for.

What does Medjugorje mean to me?

Four years after the court case, I joined a religious order in the Philippines. I spent three and a half years in the seminary there but then had to return back home due to ill health. I am currently preparing for my tenth trip to Medjugorje, bringing my fourth youth group out for the annual Youth Festival. I intend to continue my studies for the priesthood, God willing. Obviously, my journey is still ongoing and the struggles are still there but the Gospa gets me through it each day. Thank you for everything. *Totus Tuus, Maria!*

17

Pascale Gryson

BELGIUM

This is the testimony of Madame Pascale Gryson, given on 5 August 2012 in Medjugorje, following her remarkable healing (after slow and regular progression) from leukoencephalopathy, a rare and incurable disease. This occurred on 3 August 2012 during Mass, having received Communion.

The transcript of this testimony from French to English was kindly translated by Catherine Jacqué.

The interviewer puts the question to Pascale, 'Did you ask to be healed?'
I asked for healing a long time ago. It is important to realise that I had been ill for more than fourteen years. I have always been a believer – a profound believer – engaged in the service of the Lord all my life, so when the first symptoms manifested themselves, I asked and begged for healing. Other members of my family joined me in my request but an answer was not forthcoming, or at least not the response I was waiting for – but there were other responses! At one time, I said to myself that, no doubt, the Lord had other plans.

The first responses which I received were the graces to bear this illness: the grace of strength and the grace of joy. Not a constant joy but in any case a profound joy, in the depths of my soul. You might say that this small part of the soul remained filled with the joy of God, even during moments of the greatest distress.

I firmly believe that the hand of God has always rested on me. I never doubted his love for me, despite this illness, which could cause one to doubt His love for us.

A few months ago, my husband and I felt a pressing call to come to Medjugorje, without knowing what Mary had prepared for us. It was like an irresistible pull. This great call surprised me, above all because of the fact that my husband and I were both called with the same intensity. In contrast, our children remained completely indifferent, outraged as they were by my illness, rebelling against God. They kept asking me why God healed some and not others. My daughter said to me: 'Mum, why do you, who prays, not pray to be healed?' But I had accepted the illness as a gift from God, after years of decline.

I want to share with you what this illness has brought me. I don't think that I would be the person I am now without the grace of this illness. I was very sure of myself. The Lord gave me gifts of a human kind. I was a brilliant artist, very proud. I had studied literature and my progression through school had been very easy and exceptional. Everyone admired me.

In short, I think that this illness opened my heart and cleared my view, because it is an illness which touches all that you are. I had really lost everything. I reached the bottom physically and spiritually, as well as psychologically, but in my heart I could also experience and understand what others were going through.

The illness opened my heart and my understanding. I think that I was blind and now I see what others can experience. I love them. I want to help them. I want to be with them. I was also able to discover the wealth and beauty of being close to another person. Our relationship as a couple has deepened. I could never have imagined such depth.

In one word, I discovered 'love'. That of the Holy Trinity, that of Our Lady, the Mother of God, but also that of all of those close to me; all of those who were able to surround me with such tenderness.

A short while before our departure on this pilgrimage, we decided to bring our two children here with us. My daughter – I am going to say – 'ordered me' to pray for healing, not because I wished it or desired it, but because she wanted it. In the bus which brought us here to Medjugorje, she received an extract from the Gospel which told her that if she had enough faith – I cannot recall the exact words – she would heal the sick by placing her hands on them. ('These are the signs that will be associated with believers: in my name they will cast out devils; they will have the gift of tongues; they will pick up snakes in their hands and be unharmed should they drink deadly poison; they will lay their hands on the sick, who will recover' [Mark 16:17–18]).

I encouraged her, as well as my son, to ask for this grace for their mother and they did so, overcoming difficulties in belief and their rebellion. For my husband and I, this journey was an unimaginable challenge.

We left with two wheelchairs. Being unable to remain seated, a wheelchair which would recline as much as possible was required. We rented one, but our bus had no wheelchair facilities. Arms were offered again and again throughout the day to carry me, to exit, to enter.

I could never, ever forget this solidarity, which for me is the greatest sign that God exists. For all those who helped me, unable to speak, also for the welcome which I received from the organisers, for every person who made even a single effort to help me, I have begged Our Lady to grant them her special and maternal blessing.

My greatest desire was to witness the apparition of Mary to Mirjana. Our guide agreed to bring my husband and me there. There, once again, I experienced a grace which I will always remember. Several people carried me across the dense crowd in my stretcher-chair, defying the laws of possibility, to allow me to reach the place itself, the little alter which receives the apparition of Mary.

We spent many hours waiting in prayer; it seemed to me a single moment, a moment of eternity. I can tell you that at this moment we were already fulfilled by our journey to Medjugorje. A missionary nun spoke to my husband and me, repeating to us the message which Mary had intended specifically for the sick. She reminded us that Our Lady promised graces to the sick on one condition: that we be willing to offer Her our suffering in an act of faith, even thanking God for what we have to endure. For me, the three graces were light, strength and healing.

The first two are easy to understand. With regard to healing, I felt the certainty of being healed within. What I wish to speak of is really this complete, inner joy, accompanied by peace. No more rebellion! What I am also certain of since that moment, is that the Lord heals us all but this healing is progressive, quicker or slower depending upon the Lord's plans for our greater good.

It is certain that upon the day of our entry into heaven, none of us will be in a wheelchair, and I thanked God for the healing that awaited me one day or another.

The next day, Friday, 3rd of August, my husband went out in the morning to do the Way of the Cross. It was very warm and my greatest dream was to be able to accompany him. But there was no porter available and my condition was really difficult to bear. It was better for me to remain in my bed. I remember this day as one of the most painful during all of my illness.

I had to work for each breath despite the respiratory machine, the BiPAP (Bi-level Positive Airway Pressure) which had accompanied me there.

My husband had left with my blessing – I would never have wanted him to give this up. I could neither eat nor drink anything, nor take my medication. I was confined to my bed. I didn't even have the strength to pray. I was simply face to face with the Lord.

My husband returned very happy, deeply moved by the experience of the Way of the Cross. Full of compassion for me, without any explanation on my part, he understood that, for me, the Way of the Cross had taken place in my bed.

During the Way of the Cross, someone had mentioned several episodes during the life of Fr Slavko. You should know that my husband only knew of him since our journey in the bus, where he had been able to watch a film about the life of this exceptional priest.

I thought that my husband would want to rest after his trek on the mountain but, to my great surprise, he had only one idea – to bring me as soon as possible to the grave of Fr Slavko. So I allowed myself to be transported to this place, in the beginning of the afternoon, under a scorching sun. There, once again, we experienced an unforgettable moment of deep reflection, received internal graces of strength, gentleness, peace and communion.

Without consulting each other, my husband and I had expressed the same prayer:

Lord, if it is your will, let me be cured, not in part, not a little but deeply – not for ourselves as we are already so fulfilled by your Love – but for our children.

We prayed intensely for them, that God would take them under his protection and give them, first and foremost, the best lives he could give them. Gathering together the last of my strength, we decided to go to the Eucharist after the evening meal. I left without the respirator; the weight of this heavy machine upon my knees had become unbearable. We arrived late – I hardly dare say it – at the proclamation of the Gospel. We wore our headphones (which allowed us to pick up the French translation) as we 'approached' in order to pick up pieces of what was happening in our absence.

As soon as we arrived, I began to implore the Holy Spirit with a joy I cannot express. I asked Him to take possession of my whole being. I told Him of my renewed desire to belong to Him, body, soul and mind. From that moment, I no longer felt that I was on the earth.

The celebration of Mass continued until the Consecration.

Then, the moment of Communion arrived, which I had awaited intensely. My husband led me to the queue at the back of the church. A priest crossed the aisle with the Body of Christ. He came directly towards my husband and me, passing by all the other people who were waiting. We had both taken Communion, the only ones, at that time, in that line. We moved away to leave a place for the other communicants and began our acts of thanksgiving.

Then I smelled a powerful and very sweet scent, a heavenly scent. I had previously smelled a similar perfume close to icons which exuded a rose scented oil. I looked around, searching for the origins of this smell, but we were alone.

My internal eye was then focussed upon God the Father and I saw myself in spirit in white garments having just received the sacrament of reconciliation, dancing before our Father. I said to him with a little smile, 'After all ... you know well that I can't do that ... at last ... with my soul, yes! I can praise you and dance, and sing in a wholly spiritual way.'

Then I felt a strength passing through me, not a heat, but a strength. A current of life passed through the unused muscles of my legs. Then I said to God, 'Father, Son and Holy Spirit, if you are doing what I think, to bring about this unthinkable miracle, then I ask of you a sign and a grace. Let it be possible that I can communicate with my husband.'

I turned to my husband and I tried to say to him: 'Do you smell that scent?' He replied to me in the most natural way, 'No, my nose is a little blocked.' I say 'natural' because he hadn't heard my voice for a year! To wake him up I said 'Hey! I'm talking! Do you hear me?'

There, I knew that God had achieved his work and in an act of faith, I removed my feet from the wheelchair and I stood up. All the people around us realised what had just happened. One person said to me that I seemed incredibly young. I felt that I was on Mount Tabor, the Mount of the Transfiguration.

In the following days my condition improved from hour to hour. I no longer wished to sleep for hours on end and the pain caused by my illness gave way to the aches of physical efforts which had been impossible for me for seven years.

So then, this is the account which I wished to entrust to you. Now, if you have questions to ask, do not hesitate.

Some questions were put to Pascale

How did your children welcome this news?
I think the children are very, very happy but you must take into account that they have practically always known me to be ill and they will need some time to adapt to this change.

What is your illness called?
The name of my illness is leukoencephalopathy. It is a rare and incurable disease, the symptoms of which are similar to those of multiple sclerosis.

What do you want to do with your life now?
That's a very difficult question because when God offers a grace, he is also giving us an enormous responsibility. My greatest wish, which is also that of my husband, is to show ourselves faithful to the Lord, to his grace and, as much as we are able, not to disappoint Him.

So, to be really practical, what seems clear to me now is that at last I am going to be able to assume my responsibility and my life as mother and wife. That's the priority. My deep hope is also to be able to lead a life of prayer, alongside this bodily, earthly life – a life of contemplation. I would also like to be in a position to respond to all people who ask me for help, whatever it is. And equally, to testify to the love of God in our lives. It is possible that other activities will be possible for me now but I do not wish to make any decisions without profound thought, clarified by the advice of a spiritual counsellor under the eyes of God.

18

Siobhan Mhic Craith

IRELAND

Siobhan Mhic Craith is the daughter of legendary traditional Irish musician, Liam Clancy, of The Clancy Brothers fame. Although her father strayed away from his faith, and religion was not important during the early years of her family life, Siobhan's mother brought her to Medjugorje in 1989. This visit proved to be the catalyst for her conversion. When I interviewed Siobhan, she spoke openly about her strong faith and what Medjugorje means to her.

Louise: Maybe you will start by telling me a bit about your family life when you were younger and also about religion in your household and what it meant within your family.

Siobhan: My parents got married in 1966 and I was born in 1968. At that time, my father was quite a famous and well-known folk singer with both The Clancy Brothers and Tommy Makem.

My earliest memories would begin about the time he started singing with Tommy Makem as a duo. We lived in Canada and at that time we went to Catholic school. My mother and father had decided that they would like us to go to the same type of Catholic schools that they had gone to.

Both of them had pretty much lapsed in the practice of their faith, through the swinging sixties and living in New York but they had loved their faith when they were children. They loved the Mass and the devotions but the times they were living in meant they had drifted away from their faith.

However, they did want us to start off with the Catholic religion, more to give us something to rebel against when we were older than anything else. They wanted to protect us against searching for something spiritual in the wrong places, in some kind of cult or something; my father was afraid of that.

So, he was happy for us to go to Catholic school but when we would come home from school, he would try to unteach us everything that we had been taught there.

But it wasn't all doom and gloom because he really taught us to search for the truth for ourselves. We questioned everything: What was the nature of existence? Was there a God? How did the universe come about? What does life mean? Is there an afterlife? We discussed these things all the time and so we were always thinking in that sort of way.

His Catholic faith, even though he had pretty much renounced it, was always under the surface. If you listen to his music and the songs that he sang, and if you listen especially to the poetry that he chose to recite, you will see that even though he tried to get away from his Catholic faith, it was always there underneath.

There was an influence there. His outlook and his sense of charity, his sense of hope, resurrection and understanding of suffering, it was all there in a lot of his songs. That's why a lot of people find his music so inspirational and healing.

I've met lots of people who have said that listening to his singing got them through some really difficult times.

Now, I'm talking about the songs he sang more when he was working as a solo artist and working as a duo with Tommy Makem. When he sang with The Clancy Brothers there was a lot of drinking songs and rowdy songs and a lot of traditional Irish songs, which were great and good fun and everything, but as he moved on in his career, he chose to sing a lot of songs that had a deeper message. He took songs from all kinds of genres and made them his own, even contemporary songs. He sang a Paul Brady song called 'Follow On' which is lovely and he also sang a beautiful song which was written by a man from Waterford called, 'Children after the Rain,' which is about hope and new life. So he chose really good songs to sing in his later years.

Louise: What about growing up and going through the teenage years? Was your faith at the back of your head or were you trying to go to Mass and practice?

Siobhan: I would say I was pretty lost – that's how best I can describe it. I always had a sense of frustration and boredom. I would have been saying, 'Ah, the Church is ridiculous in what it teaches' and I wouldn't have taken the Church seriously. But I did have some moments myself of prayer and I did have some little bit of love for Our Lady, and a vague idea of Jesus. I would have been typically doing what everyone my age was doing, which was thinking about boys and partying when I was older in college.

Louise: Tell me about the first time you heard about Medjugorje.

Siobhan: My mother's sister had gone there in the mid-eighties. At that time, we thought it was very bizarre and we thought that it was for religious fanatics. We thought it was a bit worrying. Then my mother announced that she was going to go there with her sister and we thought 'well, that's weird but whatever you want to do'. When she came back from Medjugorje, she'd had an experience there.

It was like night turned to day in our family. Something had changed and there was a warmth and a hope that came into the family. Everything had changed, even though nothing really seemed that different. It just shows how much the mother is the heart of the home because when she changed and started to pray and started to have hope, it just changed everything in our house.

Louise: Did your mother talk to you about her experience?

Siobhan: She sure did! She told me all about her experience. I didn't disbelieve her, I believed that her experience was *her* experience but I found it all a bit hard to take in. I did listen to her; she talked a lot about Our Lady and different things. I would listen to her and take some of it in, but sometimes I would just listen to her because I felt sorry for her. I felt that somebody had to listen to her. I wanted to be polite and I didn't want to be mean or tell her to be quiet. It wasn't until after my own conversion that I realised how much I had actually learned from her and the little things she was telling me.

Louise: So did she make the suggestion that you go to Medjugorje to find out for yourself? How old were you when you went?

Siobhan: I was twenty years old and I was in college in Dublin, studying to be a Montessori teacher. I had also done a year in art college. It was actually my aunt who invited me to go and it was sort of a family pilgrimage. My grandfather had died in November and he had left her a little bit of money. She decided to use that money to bring family members to Medjugorje. She asked my mother if she thought I would like to go. My mother asked me and I said, 'Sure, I'll go.'

It was more because it was a free holiday and it was a place I had never been before. I was interested in travelling and seeing the world. I felt it would be an interesting experience and that I would go and see what was going on there. I really didn't think about what would happen to me in Medjugorje. I just felt there would be sunshine, it was Yugoslavia, I don't have to pay for this myself – sure what's a week.

Louise: When you got over there, what were your first impressions of the place?

Siobhan: Well, the trip from Spilt to Medjugorje on the bus was exciting and thrilling; it's kind of a dangerous road! And I was really excited to be in a different country and to see a different culture. There were five priests in our group, which was unusual for me because I had never been in the company of a priest before in my life, except when they were up on the altar. There was one girl my age there. I had my camera because I liked photography and I regarded myself as making a little documentary of the experience.

I was observing everything, taking pictures and trying to absorb all the landscape and scenery, as well as the characters that were on the bus. When we arrived to our B&B, my mother and I had a nice little room together. She gave me a string of rosary beads when we arrived and I took them and threw them into the closet. She said to me, 'Take these because they are blessed.' I said back to her, 'I don't believe in "blessed"! That's only symbolic,' and I threw them away.

We headed off up to the mountain where the first apparition happened and the leader of our group started praying the rosary. I was really uncomfortable with the prayers because I had never prayed like that. She asked me if I would lead a decade of the rosary and I didn't want to do that at all. I was really uncomfortable and my mother stepped in to save me and indicated to the lady that I wasn't used to this. It was dark by the time we got up onto the hill and it was very peaceful and warm, but I felt really uncomfortable with all the people there praying and so I went off on my own.

I was thinking to myself, 'What am I doing here? This is just bizarre.'

There was a crucifix on the hill and I went over and sat down at the foot of this cross.

I said, 'Jesus, I'm here and you know me and I know you,' even though I didn't know him very well. I felt more comfortable alone with Him than with the group of people who were all praying together. I had a little moment there of trusting myself to Him and then we just got on with the rest of the pilgrimage.

Louise: Were your experiences in Medjugorje the start of your conversion?

Siobhan: Well the start of my conversion probably would have happened long before I went to Medjugorje but I didn't realise that at the time. I was being prepared for it for a long time before I actually went there. I think I came to a point where I said to myself, I either believe that Our Lady is appearing here, or I don't.

From everything that happened to me, all the little different experiences, I really believed that she genuinely was appearing. And one of my thoughts was, 'Thank God I was born a Catholic, because now I don't have to go through a conversion to become a Catholic.' If she is appearing here and this is a Catholic parish, then the Catholic religion must have something to do with it and we must be on the right track.

So it started very small and I just got that conviction that if our mother is coming from heaven and she is telling us to pray and she is telling us to believe in Jesus, to go to Mass, pray the rosary, to give up things, to go to confession and to fast, then you have to do what your mother tells you.

That was my starting point.

When I got on the bus to leave, I really didn't know if I was going to totally turn my life around. I didn't expect that I was going to become a different person or anything. I was quite nervous about facing the future and didn't know what this really meant for me. I started with going to Sunday Mass and praying just one decade of the rosary a day. That was twenty-five years ago and since then, it's been a long, slow process growing a little bit every year. Sometimes it seems like it's one step forward and two steps back but I love my faith. I have made the best friends, I've had great times and great fun. I've had struggles too, and really big challenges, but I think the challenges have always made me grow more in my faith. They made my faith grow deeper and helped me to trust God more.

Louise: When your father passed away, how did your faith help you deal with that?

Siobhan: My faith helped me to deal with it because I trusted that God was there and that He was taking care of everything. I was very worried about my father because he never seemed (outwardly anyway) to have any sort of conversion. I was hoping that he would. We were praying for him all the time.

I guess we trust in God's promises. We were praying the Divine Mercy Chaplet for him. Jesus gave the Divine Mercy Chaplet to St Faustina in 1935, which is the same year that my father was born. One of the promises Jesus gave St Faustina was that if you prayed the chaplet in the presence of a dying person, that He will meet that person as a merciful saviour and not as a judge. And that even though their sins would be scarlet, they would be white as snow.

He gave that promise and so we were praying the chaplet in his company as he died. My mother was also praying the Divine Mercy Chaplet as he was dying, before the Blessed Sacrament in the chapel in the hospital. So we trust that promise and that was a source of real conversion for me. It was almost like my second conversion.

To go through my father's death with him, was something really special and it really brought my faith to life. Something wonderful happened during his funeral. My father died on a first Friday at about noon. It was the 9th of December. I remember thinking that there was something significant about dying on the first Friday.

Sometime later, when we were talking about memories, one of his sisters told us a story. She said she remembered my father coming to her house one day. He was about nineteen and she said he was full of the joys. He had just finished the nine first Fridays and he was over the moon!

I remember thinking, 'Wow, he had done that.' And then I started to look into the promises of the first Fridays. One of the promises was that the person would not be lost, that they would not die without the mercy of Jesus and His Sacred Heart. So there were two promises there that I held onto tightly.

When my father was being buried, just as they were lowering the coffin into the grave, there was a rain shower. A double rainbow came across the sky. It was really vivid and people turned around and gasped. I knew from my faith that the rainbow was a sign of God's covenant to us. It was a sign of His promise to us, that He would save us and He wouldn't destroy us. Months later, I was talking to my children about the double rainbow at their grandfather's funeral. I was talking to them about the Divine Mercy and the Sacred Heart of Jesus. One of my daughters said to me, 'yes, two promises, two rainbows!'

We make promises and we break them, but He never breaks them. That gave me so much hope and also made me want to do the nine first Fridays.

Louise: When you came back from Medjugorje and spoke to your dad about the place, what was his reaction?

Siobhan: It disturbed him a good bit, I think. It was irritating, and we had to decide in our house that we wouldn't talk about religion. He was challenged by it, but we all came to an agreement to live and let live. Let him do his thing and let us do ours. We didn't ever try to talk him round or argue with him or convince him. But I think over the years and by our example, he started to see that there was really something in what we were doing.

He always asked us to pray for him. By the time he came to his sickness, he didn't have a big conversion and turn back to God, but what he did do was turn to us. He always asked us, 'Pray for me, I know your prayers are helping.'

We come to God through one another. I don't know what it was, maybe he was too frightened and so he couldn't go directly to God himself, but he did turn to us and he knew who we were turned to.

Louise: Tell me a little bit about what you are involved in now, in terms of your faith.

Siobhan: About four years ago, I discovered this television programme called *Women of Grace* on EWTN. I was really taken with Johnnette Benkovic. I had never seen anybody who could tell the truth the way it is – the hard teachings of the Catholic Church that people are often not too keen on – with so much compassion.

I really identified with her. I had never heard anyone speak about the 'woman' the way she spoke about women. Something really resonated with me.

She has a study called the Women of Grace. There are eight chapters and it takes about nine weeks to do. I decided that this was something I could do and fit it in with life at home, as I am a stay-at-home mother. I thought it would be a bit of evangelisation work.

So, I have been facilitating that study and I am on my third one at the moment. I've just found it so fantastic. There is so much healing in it. Really, the message of Women of Grace is that it wasn't some random accident that some people are men and some people are women. To be a woman, doesn't just mean that you are a woman physically, but spiritually also.

Louise: Being a mother of three children, how do you find bringing them up in the faith, with all the pressures of modern day society?

Siobhan: It's not easy, but it's not that difficult either. Children are so receptive and so open. I just say prayers with them and we talk about our faith. If they ask me questions, I give them as much of a true answer as I can. It's hard because the world is giving them a message that's very different from the message that I would want them to receive. But they are very open to God and very open to the truth. They seem to have a natural instinct for the truth. I'm certainly not the best mother in the world – I lose my temper, I get tired and everything else – but at least they know that I love them and they know that God loves them. They know that Our Lady is there and she is a better mother than I am. They have two mothers and so where I fail, she doesn't.

Louise: What does Medjugorje mean to you?

Siobhan: I probably wouldn't have my faith at all if I didn't have that original trip to Medjugorje. Medjugorje is like a school of Our Lady. She is teaching us, and all she is really doing is pointing us to her Son who gives us everything.

Medjugorje isn't really about Our Lady at all, even though she is the one who is appearing there. Medjugorje puts you in touch with the Church and once you start to delve into the sacraments and holy scripture, then you have everything.

Medjugorje points you to Jesus, points you back to God, puts you on the right track and off you go! I went four more times after my first visit and then I went to Craig Lodge in Scotland, which is a Medjugorje-style House of Prayer where they are trying to live Our Lady's message. I lived there for five years and it was like a little Medjugorje, so I never felt the need to go back. Then I got married and had my children, so I haven't been back to Medjugorje since I got married. Hopefully, I will be able to bring my children there someday soon, please God.

19

Binni Larkin

The first time Binni Larkin says she met Our Lady was back in 1985 when she was nine years old. However, as a child, she had not been brought up with any particular religion. Between the ages of nine and twenty-nine, things happened in her life – some good, some not so good – and she 'lost touch' with Our Lady. In 2009, someone suggested she visit Medjugorje and a path was laid out before her which made it possible for her to make the pilgrimage. In 2010, she was baptised into the Catholic Church.

This is Binni's testimony.

My uncle was getting married and his wedding reception was to be held beside St Anselm's Church in London. It was autumn 1985 and I was nine years old. There was a slight chill in the air but the sun was still happily shining. Out of curiosity, I was drawn to go into the church adjacent to the hall, which my aunt and I had had a sneaky look at earlier. I remember quite clearly the peace and serenity in the vast but quiet church and Our Lady's statue some seven feet tall at the top of the altar. She was gently holding the infant Jesus in her arms. She wore a sky-blue flowing mantle, and her alabaster skin glistened, like the sun shining on the rippling ocean.

Initially, I remember feeling a little awkward being there; almost guilty for being so nosy. But I couldn't help myself, I just had to have a look! There was a young, dark-haired woman reading at one of the front pews. She was not much older than I am today. I know now she was in prayer, but I didn't understand at that time what she was doing in the quietness on her own.

My aunt, who happened to be with me, was equally interested, but her reasons for going into the church were her own. She had grown up in the area and I very much doubt she had ever set foot inside a church before then, least of all this one.

The moment I saw Our Lady on the altar I couldn't take my eyes away. I felt comforted by her kind face and strong presence. I felt warm and safe; something I hadn't felt for a very long time. I didn't want to leave. I felt light. I felt (I know this sounds crazy) that I belonged there with her. I was reluctant to leave and when I eventually did, she stayed on my mind for a considerable amount of time thereafter.

I'd dream of her frequently after that visit. Once, during a particularly turbulent time in my life, I dreamed about her as I had done many times before, only in this dream her statue moved. Her face turned slowly towards me and she smiled. Then, she looked down at the baby in her arms and she continued to smile; that warm, loving smile. It was almost as if she was telling me, with her silent smile, that she would embrace me like the child in her arms. This dream didn't frighten me or cause me distress – in fact, quite the reverse.

I awoke the following morning feeling loved and fulfilled, like my heart was going to burst with happiness. I often remember that dream. I know it was just that – 'a dream' – but it made me smile, and her smile visits me often in other ways now, through people: my family, friends, clients, children and acquaintances.

I distinctly remember that growing up, I was never alone. There was always the presence of a friend beside me all the time, every day. This feeling was particularly strong when I was troubled, less so during happier times, but there nonetheless. I didn't understand it at the time and put it down to it being like an imaginary friend as some children of that age have. I know better now, and it filled me with hope and a much better understanding of holy angels, the presence of Our Lady, and Jesus protecting and guiding us before I could understand what this presence was.

I visit my family at home in London every so often and when I do, I make a pointed effort to go to Sunday Mass at St Anselm's with my cousin. Our Lady's statue is no longer there and the church itself has changed over the years, but it was one of my earliest and most profound experiences of Our Lady and it will stay with me until my time comes to leave this world. St Anselm's Church will always have a special place in my heart.

Between the ages of nine and twenty-nine, a lot happened in my life; some good, some not so good. Somewhere along the line I lost touch with Our Lady and she didn't feature in my dreams as frequently as before. Towards the end of my twenties, I had little faith; none at all in some cases. I'd lost that special feeling a long time ago. I don't know how but I just did. I didn't visit another church again for many years.

During my mid-to-late twenties I took a job working abroad. As I arrived in the hotel room after a long journey, I was mentally and physically tired. I was fit to do little but rest. I had to ring home and let them know I had arrived safely. I tried calling my aunt but she didn't answer. I rang both my brother and sister, but they didn't answer either. I tried calling two of my superiors, neither of whom were available to take my call. I tried calling my grandmother and another aunt, again no answer. I had called seven people to let them know, to let someone know where I was and that I had arrived safely, but there wasn't anybody there to listen.

I was so upset, and I cried. I looked up and said 'I'm all alone!' At that moment in time, I realised just how alone I really was and that I could be in danger or dead and no one would know or care. I was feeling very sorry for myself. This distressed me so much. I continued to cry, then I heard a gentle thud beneath me.

I knew I was alone in the room but felt almost like something was watching me. It made me a little nervous but the sun shone so brightly through the window that I didn't think anything bad was about to happen. I could hear the lifts going up and down in the building, so I wasn't far from help if I was in any kind of trouble. I investigated under the bed and discovered an opened book. As I picked up the book I realised it was a standard copy of the bible, the type you'd find in most hotel rooms. I was drawn to read a particular verse which looked as if it had been highlighted. The passage read, 'Though my father and my mother abandon me, the Lord will hold me close' (Ps 27:10).

This psalm really does speak volumes; it doesn't require any explanation from me. What I will say is this – we human beings are so busy in our lives, that we often forget that Jesus is waiting for us to return to Him. It is our free will that gets us through our days and that same free will allows us to make the choices we do. We should be thankful for this free will and for what we have and this will guide us back to our path.

They say 'God moves in mysterious ways' but does He really have to be so dramatic and frighten the living daylights out of me, especially like that? I'm sure He knows what He is doing, because, right then and there, I felt a little happier knowing I wasn't alone. I don't see holy angels, but if you concentrate hard enough you can almost feel their presence. It's tangible. This was similar to what I'd experienced when I was younger and this presence felt stronger the more I thought about it. Ignorance is bliss, but it's only a matter of time until truth will out. I daresay if the Lord wants to make himself known through his works then there is nothing we can do about it. Just be prepared to receive whatever it is you might have asked or prayed for. Just remember to ask Him to show you gently. In this case, I cried out in momentary emotional pain, and what I received was an equally strong response, not quite what I was expecting but a response nonetheless.

In 2004, I met my husband. I'd arrived at a major crossroads in my life, where I needed to make a decision about my life and where it would go. I had two options: the easier option of the two would have led me down a very uncertain path and I shudder to think where it might have brought me. The second option wasn't as easy and required a great deal of willpower and strength I had never known before, but the result is what you see today. My husband assisted me in making decisions in my life without having to make them himself. I'm happily married and settled within myself as a person. I've never felt more in control and blessed with everything I have in my life now and that didn't come overnight. All good things come to those who wait, as I now understand.

My interest in prayer returned when I was in my mid-twenties. Things in life were going well and I felt the need to say thank you to something or someone. I reflected on what my life had been compared to what it had now become. I was healthier and happier. I was really beginning to enjoy myself and things were getting better all the time. I was feeling happier, which meant people I came into contact with felt happier too. Everybody warms to a happy person. That's my reward every day. If I can make someone smile, or do or say something that makes them happier, my heart swells.

In 2007, I decided to take my interest in faith a little further and started the RCIA (Rite of Christian Initiation of Adults), with the Spiritual Guidance of my good friend Fr Paul Thornton. Paul made this particular part of my spiritual journey instructive, educational, easy to learn and relevant to me as a person. I developed a thirst for knowledge like never before and I shall be forever grateful to him for his patience and guidance. A lot of things in my life started to fall into place and I had a better understanding of what I was supposed to be doing. This was a personal education for me and very few people knew what I was doing. I was meant to do this course a long time ago but kept putting it on the back-burner, thinking that I'd come back to it when I had more time. I had no idea I was a late bloomer until I started the course and slowly but surely I started to open my heart and mind to other avenues in my life.

In April 2009, someone suggested that I should visit Medjugorje. I had been asked to go several times before, and on every occasion up until then I had politely declined. I'd heard mixed reports of this place which all the 'holy molys' were talking about and I didn't feel the need to go. In fact, it made me a little uncomfortable. I had far better things to be doing with my time than spend it with a bunch of straight-laced, serious, old, boring people, on my knees, praying for a week. That was my idea of hell!

As I had been asked so many times before, I suppose I felt that I was being rude by not taking the time to find out what all the fuss was about. In the past, if anything had taken my interest, I would research it until I'd exhausted the subject, but in this case I had failed to do just that with Medjugorje. It just hadn't interested me much.

I had heard that the weather was glorious, the food was fresh and extremely good, the rich wine flowed, and that it was located in quite an unspoiled part of the world, all at a reasonable price. When it was put to me like that, I thought, 'What's not to like?' So I took a chance, if only to bask in the sunshine for a week and spoil myself.

I consulted my diary and, funnily enough, it opened on the exact date that I would be flying to Dubrovnik, Wednesday 8 May 2009, and returning on the 15th. This was really bizarre. During all of the weeks from the New Year up to Christmas, I had at least one entry on every page but this week was completely clear – not even a penciled-in date, which I'd often have. I remembered I had banked all the takings for the business that morning to cover various bills and expenses, so there wasn't much disposable income for the trip, but I checked my sorry-looking purse all the same. I don't know why I did that, as I knew there was little in it. What I found stopped me in my tracks. There in my purse were seven brand new, crisp notes to cover the exact cost of my trip. I still have the docket from the bank to prove I'd banked the takings. I couldn't understand how this was possible. I must've forgotten to pay a bill, or something. But there it was and so I agreed to go to Medjugorje. The decision had already been made before I said yes.

From that moment, something very strange happened – business was good and every client I saw was in great form. The weather improved and I found parking wherever I needed it. I kept to my schedule very well. I found I was very productive and spent my time wisely, ticking off an endless 'to do' list and accomplishing everything I needed to prior to my trip. Everything seemed lighter and I felt happier. Little did I know I was about to start the rollercoaster ride of my life.

To those who know me, I am happy, positive, and always good company, but this time I was even happier, so and I couldn't explain why. This continued right up until I got on the plane to take me to that place where all the 'Holy Joes' went.

The plane was full of happy, smiling people travelling to the same destination, and the magnitude of what I had agreed to finally hit me. I snapped out of this silly dream that I was going on a sun holiday, and I quickly realised that I was going to be surrounded by people who walk, talk and sleep prayer. What had I done? Remember, this was my idea of hell! I wasn't cut out for it, but there was no turning back now. I thought I would hatch a cunning plan when I landed and felt I could always do a disappearing act and no one would be any the wiser. Phew, good job I had my thinking cap on. Needless to say, that didn't happen.

The more I got talking to various people on the way there, the more I realised they were ordinary people much like me, but they all had an extraordinary excitement about them. I learned some had saved all year to come to this place and I remember being humbled by this. The least I could do was try to participate, if only a little. I would enjoy myself and make the best of a bad situation, as it were. So I did. No one knew me and I felt that I might as well get on with it. It was simple: if I didn't like it, I just wouldn't go back.

My first time in Medjugorje had such a profound effect on me and I haven't been the same since – but in a good way, I assure you. From the people I met and talked with, to the trip itself, it was a huge eye-opener. Those who shared their stories with me helped me to learn more about myself as a person, and more about Our Lady and what the apparitions were about, than I had during my entire lifetime. I also had to deal with my own issues which I had shied away from for years. They all came to the surface and I had little choice but to deal with them then. I had been caught off guard, but I had to shake it all off and this was clearly the place to do it.

On reflection, I see that this was Our Lady's way of helping me clear away all that hurt and guilt I had been carrying around all my life. It was a bit like a ball and chain stopping me from progressing. It took me a while but I can see now that Our Lady wants to help and that she loves us tenderly.

Coming away from Medjugorje, I had experienced every emotion possible, from hurt, anger, despair and self-hatred, to forgiveness, tolerance, understanding, patience and, ultimately, love. Whatever lesson I was supposed to learn, I think I covered them all in record time. If you haven't been to Medjugorje, you should go there and make up your own mind, but be prepared, as you never know what you might come away with. I certainly didn't bargain on getting a whole life-lesson in one week, that's for sure.

Adoration in Medjugorje is one of the most special moments, where even words are inadequate to describe the peace and tranquility one feels. You could be sitting amongst complete strangers, praying the rosary in unison or silently praying for your own intentions. Like me, you might just want to appreciate the warm feeling of being in the presence of the Holy Sacrament of the Altar. It feels like such a privilege to sit in the presence of something so important. One of my few regrets in life is that it took certain turning points in my life to realise what I could've had all along, but had chosen not to. Even spending an hour in silence adoring can have a huge impact on your life and it's definitely worth a try. I tried it and I now look forward to it, as it's one of the few times I will sit quietly, doing nothing but absorbing invisible rays of happiness and love from the source itself. It doesn't cost anything but a few moments of your time and things improve beyond recognition, as they did for me.

During the trip, I had to climb Apparition Hill, as it was part of the agenda. I looked up at it with dread, thinking, 'I'm so unfit, I'm not going to be able to do it.' I was afraid I was going to stumble and make a fool of myself. As I started the walk up the hill one beautifully sunny day, I noticed an elderly lady ahead. She was absolutely ancient, as far as I could see, and she made it look so easy. I thought 'this'll be easier than I thought' and I flew up Apparition Hill. I saw people walking up the hill in their bare feet, but thought, 'How disgusting, who knows what's been there?'

Today, I understand that it is a mark of respect for Our Lady. It is people climbing Apparition Hill for a reason beyond our own comprehension. To feel a little uncomfortable deliberately is a bit like having a small taste of the crucifixion. If Jesus suffered, then we too can have a small insight into this pain in other ways. I was extremely proud of my efforts and could quite happily have done it all over again.

There were several other unusual things that happened to me in Medjugorje, but I got used to them in an accepting kind of way. One morning, there was a shadow of the crucifixion at the bottom of my bed in the house I was staying in. The blinds were tightly shut and the curtains drawn, so I couldn't find where the light, if any, was coming from. Nevertheless, it was there, and there was no reasonable explanation as to how this light was casting the shadow. I doubt myself every time I think of it.

On the way to Mass at St James' Church, I stopped at the statue of Our Lady within the grounds of the church. The statue is pure white, fresh and clean looking and there is something reassuring about it. Lots of people were jostling around, going about their own business, and as I stood there looking at the statue, I got a scent of flowers. To me, it smelt like fragrant roses, and it melted my heart. It was not the type of scent from flowers you would buy in a florist, but a wholesome, rich, liquid scent. It made me smile but I didn't give it a second thought until the same thing happened again the following day, at the same place. This time, I thought I'd taken leave of what little senses I had left. You look for a logical explanation in situations such as this. I thought perhaps I was close to a florist or rose garden, but it appeared that there wasn't one for miles!

I came back from this first trip to Medjugorje humbled and educated in a way I would never have dreamed. I'm so glad I went, and everything I asked and prayed for, I have today, and I am grateful beyond words.

In April 2010, I had successfully completed the RCIA course and was officially accepted into my local parish, St Sylvester's. My godparents still support me, emotionally and spiritually, to this day, as do my friends and family. My baptism was a huge success in more ways than one, and it happened at exactly the right time in my life.

My second trip to Medjugorje came exactly a year later between the 12th and the 19th of May 2010. Note that both trips were made during the month of May, which I have since learned is the month of Our Lady – quite appropriate.

I travelled on my own this time and met many new people on the trip from all over Ireland. I was never alone and there was always something going on and something to do. I remember the climb to Apparition Hill. I felt a bit cocky at the time; I'd done this before and I knew I could climb the hill quickly and easily. This couldn't have been further from the truth. Although I was a lot fitter this time, I struggled getting up the hill. It took me twice as long and I found it difficult. By the time I had reached the top, I was rather out of breath and it was getting dark.

For those of you who haven't done this climb, the stones and clay have a reddish hue, almost sandy. You need to look out for your next step before taking it and make sure the stones are secure before you climb to the next one. It's not impossible but it does require some patience and sturdiness. When I did arrive at the top, there were hundreds of beautifully-lit candles scattered around, and it looked so romantic and inviting. I remember various clusters of people praying the rosary softly in the early evening in different languages, but they were so quiet and softly spoken, you could almost pray along with them in English.

I understand now how the Holy Spirit was, and still is, very much active in my life. As a result, it has encouraged me to educate myself and my soul, spiritually. I did this following various pilgrimages, adoration and attending relevant services in church, whether it be Mass or talks. I know this works for me. Everything I have ever asked for since I've become close to Our Lady, I have received. The only time I don't is if it's not meant for me. This shows my tolerance and acceptance of all things I have asked for. It's nice to say that ninety per cent of my prayers are answered quickly and gently.

I've since visited Lough Derg three times, Knock twice, travelled the length of Italy and, most important of them all, visited Israel. These trips to holy places have educated me further in other areas of my life and increased my understanding of myself as well as others.

If I could, I'd visit every single place on earth where Our Lady and Jesus visited, but as I've become spiritually stronger, I've realised you don't have to go anywhere at all. You could be on your own or in a crowd, in silence or noise. It doesn't matter where you are. I just remind myself of that presence I felt as a child and think of myself as a child of God. I know in my heart that I always have great company beside me, whether I can physically see them or not. I know that I, like many others, just need to believe.

20

Amor Tenerowicz

Philippines/USA

Amor Tenerowicz is originally from the Philippines. She was left broken-hearted when a relationship with her childhood sweetheart didn't go according to plan. When she was living in the US, she heard about Medjugorje and travelled to the village in 1988. Whilst there, she had a very visual experience on Mount Krizevac.

This is Amor's testimony.

My name is Amor Tenerowicz and I am a fifty-six-year-old Filipina. When I went to Medjugorje, I was thirty years old. I was healing from a recent break-up from my childhood boyfriend, who also came from the Philippines. As a young girl, it was all I dreamed about – being married to this person someday.

I immigrated to the United States when I was nineteen years old but I still did not forget that goal. To make a long story short, when I became a US citizen I went back to the Philippines to pursue my plan.

My boyfriend and I met and started writing letters but that eventually became emotionally taxing because he would not write to me as often as I would have liked. As difficult as it was to admit, the relationship was not really there between the two of us. I was broken-hearted that my lifelong plan of marrying my childhood love was not happening and I decided to break up with him.

I discovered a Catholic charismatic prayer group and I started to attend. It was there that I first heard about trips to Medjugorje. I think Medjugorje made me realise that I could plan my life all I wanted, but that I would need to consult the Lord first. Previously, I did everything on my own, without asking God what His plans for my life were.

I was proud. I had forgotten about Him. I had always gone to Mass, but I realised that Jesus was not really number one in my life – my preoccupation was my childhood love. Medjugorje made me make Jesus my first priority. I knew He needed to be my first love, first and foremost.

Since then, God has given me a wonderful American husband of Polish/Scotch–Irish decent (I could not have found a better one – he is heaven-sent!) and a wonderful daughter.

So, I would like to share my experience of Medjugorje.

On 26 March 1988, Aurora, my pilgrimage roommate, and I decided to climb Mount Krizevac. I felt it was best to climb on the Saturday so as not to do a very strenuous climb on the Sabbath day. At about 2 p.m., we started out on our way to the mountain from Ivan's house. I began praying the rosary. The climb was a difficult one, as the trail was so rugged and steep. We also prayed the Stations of the Cross at the mountain.

When we finally arrived to the top, it was very close to the time of the apparition. For our first two days in Medjugorje, it never entered my mind to look at the sun, even though I had heard different stories about it before I left California.

However, on this occasion, I thought that since I was already outdoors I might as well look at the sun during the time of the apparition. I was told that this is when the dancing sun is usually seen.

I happened to find a rock where I could comfortably sit and rest my back on the cement surround at the base of the big cross.

I started to look at the sun; it was normal, bright and yellow. It hurt my eyes so I took my gaze off. I looked again and a light grey cloud went over the sun. This made me happy because it became easier for me to look. Then, from out of the grey cloud, came a perfect triangle, which was as bright as the sun and it did not hurt my eyes.

While this was happening, I was questioning God in my mind, asking him, 'God, am I just imagining this?' When it disappeared, the sun came back out, white like the moon.

Inside the moon was a figure of a dove, with its head pointing towards heaven and its wings spread out. The dove looked like it was outlined with a white neon light. The outline was brighter than the moon. Then, the dove assumed a different position: it reappeared with its head pointing towards the earth, with its wings still spread out.

After this, it assumed a flying position and I saw the wings moving. Just then, a big cross appeared over the sun, the beams spanning the width and length of the sun and it looked as if there were white fluorescent lights covering all four corners of each beam. It was see through, and the blue sky and the sun were visible through the beams.

The cross disappeared momentarily, before reappearing at an angle facing my left side, but I could still see it entirely. After this, the vision ceased. The sun came out as before, bright and yellow. Realising it was over, I ran with excitement to my companion, who was praying on the other side of the cross, and I told her what I had just experienced.

I went back to where I had been sitting and tested my eyes by reading from a book, in case they had been damaged in any way. A few minutes later, a lady from Trinidad and Tobago gestured to me and asked if I could take her picture. We started talking, and minutes later she suggested that I meet this young gentleman, Nathan, whom she had met at the village house where they were being accommodated. She called to him from the back of the big cross. He was around twenty years of age and was from Tennessee. After she introduced me to him, she started talking about what she experienced with the sun when they were at the Apparition Hill.

Since she was sharing her own experience, I openly shared what had just happened to me moments ago. When I got to the part about the cross, Nathan, exclaimed, 'Yes, Yes!' He was so thrilled that he hugged me. He had seen the same cross that I saw. I was very thankful to the Lord, for He gave me Nathan to confirm that what I saw was real. It was not just my imagination after all and I drew these visions when I got back to the bungalow that night. These were my experiences of Medjugorje.

21

Fr Frank Reburn

IRELAND

Fr Frank first visited Medjugorje in 1987, but was very cynical about the place and he did not have a good experience there. Twenty-six years later, he felt a strong pull to go back to the village. Even though he journeyed there on a personal retreat, he found himself unable to ignore the large numbers of pilgrims queuing up for confession. In his testimony, Fr Frank talks about the sacrament of reconciliation in a place which is known as the confessional of the world.

This is Fr Frank's testimony.

My first trip to Medjugorje was in 1987. At that stage I was only ordained a little over a year. It was not a good experience. I came away somewhat cynical and critical of what I had seen and had witnessed. Over the years, life can teach us that the problem is not always on the outside, but on be inside. The problem was with me.

I didn't return to Medjugorje again until 2013. For some very strong reason, I felt that Mary was inviting me back. One can only ignore one's mother for so long. Mothers, if nothing else, can be very persistent. I ran out of places to hide and excuses soon dried up. Because of the generosity and goodness of others, I found myself on a flight heading to Medjugorje. This time it was different. I was not leading a group. I was not going to work. I was simply going as a pilgrim; I was anonymous. This was to be my annual priestly retreat.

On arrival, the first thing I did was to go to confession. A wonderful sacrament, but, for some people, it can be a very nerve-wracking experience. I smile when I think of the words of Pope Francis, where he reminds us that the confessional is not a 'torture chamber'. More than once as a penitent, my experience of the sacrament left a bitter taste in my mouth. I wonder how many people have had the same experience, coming out of the confessional embittered and hurt.

The elderly priest who heard my confession in Medjugorje did so with great love and pastoral care. It was a wonderful, grace-filled experience; just as it should be. I found it very healing to truly bear my soul. This ritual purification led me to find rest in the bosom of God. On leaving the confessional, I encountered lines and lines of English-speaking pilgrims waiting for confession. How could I deprive them of this opportunity? I had no intentions of doing anything. I was on retreat, and this was my own time off but …

I presented my celebrate, got a pass, put on a stole and found myself spending hours and hours journeying with people in the confessional, helping others to rediscover the beauty of God's love. It was not long before I discovered that in Medjugorje, there are no secrets and no dark places. People wanted so much to share every-thing about their lives, the good and the not-so-good.

What is it about Medjugorje that brings people from near and far and gives them the courage and strength to bear their souls and open their hearts to God? It was as if the beauty of Mary's love was illuminating the dark recesses of our hearts. In the presence of such beauty, we become acutely aware of the ugliness of sin – something we wish to eliminate from our lives. It seems that, for many, Medjugorje provides the opportunity for this to happen.

So many people have rediscovered their faith in Medjugorje and, after so many years, find the courage to enter the confessional and bear their souls before God. I found the whole experience incredibly humbling; myself and others – sharing pain, journeying together, being healed. There is an honesty about Medjugorje that is reinvigor-ating. Fr Liam Lawton stated, in Louise's first book, that in Medjugorje 'many priests have rediscovered their vocation'. I believe this to be true.

We get caught up in administration, other things distract us, and prayer can be pushed aside. We become impatient, always in a hurry and moving on to the next thing. In Medjugorje, I found myself slowing down. By sitting in the confessional and helping others to be healed, you become aware, in a very strong way, of the power of healing through God's love. So many times, my thoughts were, 'This is my ministry; this is what I have been called to do.' Mary brings Jesus to us and brings *us* to Jesus, if we let Her, but so much can get in the way.

Whilst in Medjugorje, I spent hours sitting in the fields, around the church, or on Cross Mountain, sometimes praying, sometimes thinking, and always in silence. On more than one occasion my thoughts were interrupted by people asking, 'Are you a priest? Do you speak English? Would you mind if I spoke with you?' Sometimes the conversation would last ten minutes, other times it could go on for an hour; people hurting, broken, seeking, searching, but always trusting.

There is a wonderful generosity of heart in Medjugorje. As I received, I wanted so much to give. All I had as a priest was my time and that is what I gave, hopefully with a smiling heart.

There are many stories about Medjugorje. Different people have different experiences. For me, one beautiful experience was the holy hour. On my first evening, I was overwhelmed seeing so many people in one place, in the presence of the Blessed Sacrament, being led in prayer and praying silently. There is something very deep and comforting about being in the presence of so many people as the Blessed Sacrament is venerated.

I found that to close my eyes and open my heart in company, in prayer, during that holy hour, was deeply comforting. As I prayed for others, others prayed for me – a ground-swell of prayer. There were times when my mind was all over the place, and it was hard to be still. It was then that the serenity of so many people praying brought calmness into my life. Was this the 'peace' in Medjugorje that so many people talk about?

In Medjugorje, I was in the presence of people like myself, who were genuinely seeking a deeper relationship with Christ. Mary does just that; she leads us to her son. Some will say, 'But you do not need Medjugorje for that' and perhaps they are right. But being in the presence of so many who have travelled from all over the world, in a place that requires a bit of effort to get to, somehow manages to fine-tune your senses until your focus is on God.

What does Medjugorje mean to me?

It is a place where one finds peace, prayer and companionship. Through our beloved mother we are drawn into a deeper relationship with God.

22

Paolo Gambi

ITALY

Paolo Gambi is an Italian life coach, author and journalist. He has written more than twenty successful books about religion, psychology, personal development and spirituality. He is also a contributing editor to the Catholic Herald *of London. Paolo was very sceptical of the Medjugorje phenomenon but his cynical curiosity saw him visiting the village and spending three days there in 2010.*

This is Paolo's testimony

At the moment, I don't know what Medjugorje means for the Church and the world. But I do know what it means to me. We are all waiting for the official response of the hierarchy to have a better and deeper understanding of the marvellous things that have been taking place there for so many years. We shall soon understand if the hand of God is working there, or if it is something else that is happening in that place.

Many people visit Medjugorje every day. Some of them are driven by curiosity; some of them follow one of the many celebrities that appear on Italian television, talking about Medjugorje. I personally dislike this. I cannot read celebrities' hearts, so I cannot measure their sincerity. But too many of them have found in Medjugorje a way to be invited onto talk shows and TV programmes where they were not welcome anymore. Is it just a coincidence?

Regardless, this is not the central talking point of Medjugorje. Medjugorje has, in fact, become a very popular phenomenon in Italy. Italians' devotions follow unpredictable routes. Just think about St Pius of Pietrelcina, the Franciscan friar with the stigmata, who died in 1968. Maybe somebody remembers his story?

The hierarchy was very doubtful about him, about the miracles he performed, about his mystical life and his stigmata. But thousands of people visited him every day, and he was proclaimed a saint of the Catholic Church in 2002. Who knows if Medjugorje will have the same happy ending or not? And who knows if we will have to wait thirty years more to find out?

What I can assuredly say is that many people have gained a deeper faith after visiting Medjugorje. I am one of them. I spent three days in Medjugorje in 2010. I was already a devout, sinning Catholic, needing something more at that point of my life. But I was very sceptical about the Medjugorje phenomenon before my visit.

Driven by a somewhat cynical curiosity, I went to Medjugorje with a friend, Diego Manetti, who had been there fifteen times before and had co-written (with Fr Livio Fanzaga) a book about the shrine. For the whole car journey, there was a constant dialogue between my mind and his heart. I could not understand with my brain what my friend was trying to share through his heart. In the car with us, there was also my mother, as well as a boy who was searching for himself. We had all had struggles between our minds and our hearts.

Before my visit, I found it difficult to believe that Our Lady had been continually speaking for almost thirty years in such a remote part of the world. Why did she choose such a meaningless town? Someone probably asked the same thing when they realised Jesus was born in Bethlehem and not in Rome. What's more, I could not accept that Mary would be appearing on earth again to share some secrets about the trials humanity will face in the future.

Having since thought about this, I have reached the conclusion that Medjugorje is completely illogical – if you look at it in a purely rationalistic way. But, as soon as I arrived, I stepped out of a 'kingdom of reason' and into an 'empire of the heart'.

Actually, I must confess, I still find these things very hard to grasp rationally. The 'secrets' are the point at which I cannot totally enter into the Medjugorje phenomenon. I visited Sr Elvira's community, where people with drug addiction problems found a way to live normally again. I have heard the stories of some of these people, who had been through hell and who had started a new life thanks to this nun. I encountered a local man, Michele Vasilj (almost everybody who has been in Medjugorje knows him), in whose eyes I caught a glimpse of Mary's sight. I met Sr Cornelia at the orphanage she runs, and there I was given a mysterious sort of prophecy regarding my private life. It was incredible. I have not unveiled it to anybody but the person that was mentioned in it. Only after some years, and after that person had died, am I beginning to understand the meaning of that prophecy.

I cried without reason while I was praying in the parish church. I have cried only once before like this. It happened when I prayed for the first time in a charismatic community called Rinnovamento nello Spirito in Italy. But this time, my tears were much heavier and more meaningful, a gift from Our Lady. I have heard many people are gifted with tears. Maybe others will understand when I say that what happens inside you when you are experiencing those kind of tears cannot be described through human words. I listened to the visionary Mirjana recounting her experience, and I realised that some of the words she was saying from the balcony of her tiny house, in front of about a hundred people, were spoken directly to me.

When I listened to one of Mary's messages, I realised the words spoke directly to my heart, giving me the solution to a problem I had been carrying around like a heavy burden. Have I just convinced myself that this was the case? Who knows? God writes straight, but also with crooked lines. Since my visit, I have prayed three rosaries every day for three years. I had never thought about doing it before.

Even if everything was false, the visionaries were all impostors and Our Lady had never thought about going to speak to special people in Medjugorje, I could at least say that my trip has been useful for my soul. At that time, I wrote a piece for the *Catholic Herald* of London, stating how, as a journalist, I had never felt so useless before. For the first time in my career, I realised that my words were not able to express what I wanted to share. After some years, I can still say exactly the same thing.

Call me unskilled or incompetent if you want, but, when I try to describe what I have found inside me since my visit to the town, I cannot find the words. When we reach the mystery we carry inside, we can only contemplate it. And this is exactly why I find it useless to write or speak about Medjugorje, or about any other mystical experience. We cannot share the experience of our heart through the words of our mind. Or at least, if that is possible, I am not able to succeed. Are you?

After that article, many people from the USA, India, Australia and many more countries contacted me to ask me for more information about Medjugorje. I was very happy to contribute to their search. I found myself in a sort of community of people who had experienced the same thing as I had, or who were called to do it. Many of you are probably thinking, 'He is pathetic.' That is what I used to think whenever I bumped into one of the many Medjugorje devotees. Sometimes I still do, when mere reason gains the upper hand. Reason cannot grasp this phenomenon – at least mine can't. Reason is inclined to say that Medjugorje relies on coincidence, autosuggestion and emotionalism. But these explanations no longer satisfy me.

If you have experienced what I did, you would understand why. In fact, the point of my trip to Medjugorje had been precisely this: to rediscover that there is a mysterious spiritual dimension that is far beyond our understanding, which cannot be limited by our mind. So the only words that can be useful are these: go and see. In Medjugorje, a new world could be unveiled inside you. At least, that is what has happened to me.